Empowered Students

Empowered Students

Educating Flexible Minds for a Flexible Future

Kerry Decker Rutishauser

ROWMAN & LITTLEFIELD
Lanham • Boulder • New York • London

Published by Rowman & Littlefield
An imprint of The Rowman & Littlefield Publishing Group, Inc.
4501 Forbes Boulevard, Suite 200, Lanham, Maryland 20706
www.rowman.com

6 Tinworth Street, London SE11 5AL, United Kingdom

British Library Cataloguing in Publication Information Available

Library of Congress Control Number: 2020946620

ISBN 978-1-4758-5835-8 (cloth : alk. paper)
ISBN 978-1-4758-5836-5 (pbk. : alk. paper)
ISBN 978-1-4758-5837-2 (electronic)

∞ ™ The paper used in this publication meets the minimum requirements of American National Standard for Information Sciences Permanence of Paper for Printed Library Materials, ANSI/NISO Z39.48-1992.

This book is dedicated to:

Children and communities, pedagogues and scholars, thinkers and actors, innovative practice and rich theory, pedagogy and freedom, writers and self-critical reflection, critical consciousness and belonging.

Contents

Acknowledgments

To Cynthia McCallister, associate professor at New York University. Our long partnership influenced my formation and expertise as a learner-driven school educator. You gave me advice on how to start writing this book by interviewing the teachers and students at Green Careers. As a result, the teachers and student voices tell this story. Thank you.

To my husband, Michael Rutishauser, you read my first few chapter drafts and simply said, "Keep writing." Those were all the words I needed to hear. Thank you, my love, for all that you did to make this book possible by keeping our four young children always in tow.

Thank you, Margaret Watkinson, Kristen Holt Browning, Heather Terrill Stotts, Jim Rickabaugh, and Curtis Johnson for all your guidance and help to usher this book into the public consciousness.

My deepest thanks go to my editor at Rowman and Littlefield, Inc. Thank you for seeing the value and need for such a book and for taking a risk on a first-time author.

To the teachers, coaches, and principals who joined my Sunday writing shares over the course of three years to help me organize all my vignettes, thoughts, interviews, and theory core into coherent words on the page: Whitney Fink, Jeanne Zonneveld, Dan Grenell, Madeleine Cilliotta-Young, Naina Abowd, Jon Green, Chris Sedita, Luke Janka, and Elisaul Cruz. Your voices are woven into the fabric of this entire manuscript.

To Jon Green and Shannon Curran, former Network Leaders, and Richard Kahan, founder and CEO at the Urban Assembly, and to the New York City Department of Education. Thank you for your support and confidence in my leadership.

To all my fellow educators I have worked with over the past twenty-four years, from Villa Park, Illinois, to The American School of Kuwait in Kuwait City; from the Jacob August Riis School in the Lower Eastside of Manhattan to Neenah/Menasha, Wisconsin; from The Urban Assembly to The Urban Assembly School for Green Careers. Each of you contributed to my formation as an innovative educator, and many of you shared stories for this book.

Lastly and especially, thanks to the children at The Urban Assembly School for Green Careers. Thank you for your interviews and for your sincerity.

Introduction

In 2013, The Urban Assembly School for Green Careers (hereafter, "Green") High School ranked in the bottom 1 percent of New York City schools, with a 39 percent graduation rate. It had earned an "F" on the most recent citywide "School Progress Report," and violent student altercations were a regular occurrence throughout the school.

Even though the school is located on Manhattan's well-off Upper West Side, this public school was composed of students who were disadvantaged economically and struggled academically. Green was and still is a segregated, unscreened high school serving the lowest baseline of students in New York City. 95.6 percent of the students were Black or Hispanic. Nearly a quarter of the student body qualified for Special Education, another quarter qualified as Multilingual Learners (ML), and *the entire school population* averaged a second to third grade reading level. That's right: The majority of students read six to seven years below grade level.

Within weeks of taking the helm, the school's new principal worked with teachers and staff to put in place radical ideas that shifted the power dynamics around the key areas of discipline, autonomy, and voice (both written and spoken). Importantly, *she implemented these radical ideas not in a wealthy, suburban, white private school but in a segregated, urban, economically disadvantaged school.*

Empowered Students is a story based in the real world, and it is a story of how theory can be implemented as a successful practice. It dives deeply into the practical ways students at Green were released from years of oppressive schooling practices. It's about how students who entered high school reading at a second-grade level graduated just a few years later that were ready for the twenty-first-century marketplace.

Empowered Students is a well-documented and researched book. It is written about the key methods, the main players, and the educational environment in which the chief author of this book, Kerry Decker Rutishauser, worked as the principal at the time the story takes place. This is a story about self-determination and resurrection. It is about how to treat students like equal human beings who have minds of their own and how to train teachers to recognize and respond to the humanity of their students. It's a story of how the principal and the teachers did this with kids in New York City that nobody else wanted.

The kids at Green learned how to help pull each other out of cycles of oppressive teaching and discipline practices and the resulting failure—and in so doing, the students surpassed anyone's expectations. The teachers and the principal worked together to flip the traditional power structures at the school. It took a novel effort by the staff, but in the end, it was the students themselves who changed the school.

This book includes vignettes, anecdotes, testimonials, and interviews with both teachers and students that emphasize the practical effects of this approach on real people. It offers an inventive and creative, yet pragmatic, blueprint for schools to recreate and reinvent themselves. After reading this book, educators will understand how to implement an education plan that emphasizes the freedom of children's minds and voices that are at the core of every action taken.

By the end of 2016, just three years after Decker became the principal, Green had scored a perfect score on the City's "Quality Review." In 2017, Green measured as a "high impact" school: It raised its four-year graduation rate from 39 percent to 83 percent, which is 10 percent higher than comparison group averages and 9 percent higher than the city average. The Special Education graduation rate at Green was 73 percent—13 percent higher than the city average. The ML (or ELL) graduation rate was 75 percent, which is 10 percent higher than the city average. *The overall graduation rate increased by 108 percent in five years.*

PRINCIPLES OF FREEDOM

The approach presented throughout this book is grounded in the Five Principles of Freedom, a practical and theoretical framework created by Kerry Decker. This book clearly explains how schools can implement the Five Principles of Freedom to create flexible learning formats that support discipline, autonomy, and responsibility, while also encouraging freedom of mind, as outcomes. The principles are described in-depth in subsequent chapters, but they can be summarized as follows:

- *Build*: Teach kids how to build a culture of "we-ness."[1] By knowing their responsibilities to each other and entering into agreements (i.e., contracting) with other people, students build a tight-knit community.
- *Think*: Teach kids how to balance freedom and self-control. A pedagogy of freedom is about teaching students how to bring their own mental abilities under control.
- *Speak*: Teach students how to liberate their voices. When you liberate a person's voice, you liberate their thinking. Language is the very medium for thinking.
- *Act*: Teach students how to act intentionally—that is, so that their actions are within their own control rather than dictated by another. Acting intentionally allows students to learn how to behave with autonomy, control information, and create their own selfhood.
- *Fight*: Teach students how to stand up to tyranny. Freedom must always be pursued and protected constantly.

Administrators at struggling or underfunded schools, especially in poor segregated settings, will learn here how to create a safe and academically challenging learning environment. This book will empower teachers to trust themselves and their students, administrators to trust that teachers can and will change if they believe in the students—and students to trust that they can make mistakes yet still develop their voices and their abilities.

AN EXAMPLE OF GROUP AUTONOMY: COOPERATIVE UNISON READING®[2]

For example, students at Green developed their own unique identities through intentional, goal-driven, and cooperative actions. To meet their goals, students selected their own texts in genres and topics of their choosing and read them cooperatively in groups of five in every single course. While reading these self-chosen texts, students stopped the group (i.e., "breached," which is another key concept that is illustrated in-depth in the book) whenever they either recognized any confusion on their part or on the part of another student or had an insight about the text.

Once stopped, the group would exchange information until the group came to a common understanding or a precise definition of what the author's words *meant* to say to the supposed reader.[3] These tactics are part of the Cooperative Unison Reading® method, which Principal Decker first helped develop and implement earlier in her career when she was a principal at the Jacob Riis School in lower Manhattan (her experience at Jacob Riis is described in more detail in chapter 1).[4] Since reading and thinking critically and cooperatively is a difficult thing to learn how to do, Decker fiercely protected this approach to learning.

In every class, students had an opportunity to engage in interpretive discourse for a minimum of fifteen to twenty minutes per class, which amounted to students spending about 350 minutes a week engaged in critical thinking. Students learned how to analyze their own thinking processes, took actions based on their own ideas, and discussed and interpreted their own ideas as well as those of other students through both spoken and written discourse. This allowed students to learn how to exchange ideas with others and interpret the meaning of "what was said" or what was not said by the author.[5]

Developing and using these interpretive skills is essential to having a nation of thoughtful citizens who are capable of seeing themselves as solutions to the problems and issues we face.

REJECTING THE SAVIOR PERSONA

The authors of this book understand that, perhaps unconsciously, teachers and administrators may be wedded to the idea of being the "expert," dictating from the front of the classroom. Teachers often sometimes unwittingly adopt a "savior" persona, seeing children through a deficit lens and wanting to fill in their knowledge gaps, heal them, and be the one who makes a student feel more fully human. Or, very understandably, administrators working in a chaotic and unsettled school environment might be reluctant to embrace an educational philosophy centered around the concept of offering students more freedom.

It is also understood that adopting a freedom-oriented perspective requires a great amount of courage—and support. This book recognizes and sympathizes with all of these well-meaning, yet ultimately harmful, perspectives and concerns, and it explains how and why a student-freedom–focused approach works better.

DEFINING FREEDOM

"Freedom" will be defined throughout this book in greater detail, but a quick note up front about the term is required here. The word "freedom" doesn't mean the freedom to act out, disrupt class, disrespect others, or do whatever one wants at any given moment. This book is not advocating an approach that gives students free rein to do anything they want and, thus, undermines teacher authority.

Rather, "freedom" means that students learn the responsibilities that come with autonomy and self-determination. As psychologist Edmund Gordon explained on a visit to Green, "Increasing the disposition to think in pedagogy should be a balance between freedom and control since real freedom comes from the ability to bring one's own mental abilities under control." This goes back to a fundamental American concept famously articulated by Eleanor Roosevelt: "With freedom comes responsibility."

Empowered Students will hopefully convince readers that freeing children's minds in school will not only allow students to form their own unique personal identities and become fully human but to also do well on state-mandated tests and gain the skills needed to succeed in the twenty-first-century workforce. The evidence for these assertions lies in the fact that this approach was successfully implemented in a failing school with the lowest baseline of student-achievement metrics and behaviors.

The diversity of stories, voices, and perspectives in this book will emphasize that this kind of school turnaround is absolutely a team effort. Success isn't a top-down effort—for a school to succeed, the principal, teachers, staff, and students all have incredibly important work to do and roles to play.

In at least a small way, this book will help people nourish and protect public schools. The principal, teachers, staff, and students at Green together carried out this program of educational innovation within the culture of a high-accountability public school system. Public schools are under attack and must keep their enrollments up, with student bodies that represent the entire community. This book is intended to empower people who work in the public school system to be drivers of innovation so that more kids stay in, and thrive in, public schools.

NOTES

1. Michael Tomasello, *Why We Cooperate* (Boston: MIT Press, 2009) and Michael Tomasello, *Becoming Human: A Theory of Ontogeny* (Cambridge, MA and London, England: Harvard University Press, 2019).

2. Cynthia McCallister, *Unison Reading: Social Inclusive Group Instruction for Equity and Achievement* (New York: Corwin Press, 2011).

3. The "supposed reader" refers to what David R. Olson describes as the "putative reader," which is the "reader being modeled is not simply the reader him or herself, but a model of some historical or hypothetical reader." David R. Olson, *The World on Paper: The Conceptual and Cognitive Implications of Writing and Reading* (Cambridge, UK: Cambridge University Press, 1996), 156.

4. McCallister, *Unison Reading.*

5. Olson, *The World on Paper*, 93, 128–30.

Chapter One

Historical Context

In the twenty-first century, as traditional jobs and tasks are increasingly digitized and mechanized, it is more vital than ever that the uniquely human abilities to interpret, work communally, think critically, and feel empathy and sympathy be cultivated in the American educational system. Teachers are undoubtedly overworked and pressed for time—but it is critical that, rather than falling back on standard received practice, teachers readjust their pedagogical approach to focus on student freedom, initiative, and self-agency. As will be shown throughout this book, this can be accomplished without spending additional money or hiring additional teachers.

In New York City, under Mayor Bloomberg, a number of educational reforms were carried out, including the dissolution of large schools into smaller ones oriented around specific issues or disciplines. In 2009, the Urban Assembly School for Green Careers was opened as a part of this program of reform. It was one of three schools formed from Brandeis High School, a large, underperforming school. Green was designated as an unscreened school, meaning it would take those Brandeis students not accepted elsewhere, as well as any other students across the city who were not accepted into their top-choice schools.

Green's administration implemented a variety of internship, mentoring, and curriculum-support programs. Even so, by 2013, the school still rated in the bottom 1 percent of New York City schools, with a 39 percent graduation rate and an F on the School Progress Report of 2012–13.

At the request of the teachers at Green, the Urban Assembly reached out to a principal who had implemented innovative pedagogical approaches in another New York City school, with impressive results. Her approach was informed by an experience early in her career, when she had observed a second-grade class dominated by leveled reading and teacher-directed learning—and this at a progressive school, one which did not rely on worksheets and rote learning. Even in this forward-thinking environment, student voices and initiative were suppressed.

After this formative experience, as the principal of an underperforming school on Manhattan's Lower East Side, she and another education scholar had teamed up to devise an entire pedagogy centered on the core value of student intentionality. They drew on the psychological concept of Theory of Mind, as well as up-to-date conceptions of literacy acquisition, to create their own student-driven, teacher-supported educational program.

For example, they created and put in place Cooperative Unison Reading®,[1] *in which students choose a text to read as a group, read it out loud together, and discuss it as they read. Low-performing, special-needs students who practiced Cooperative Unison Reading®*[2] *saw tangible improvements in not only their literacy levels, but their overall critical-thinking skills.*

Since that early exposure to standard pedagogical practices, the principal had vowed to center student autonomy and voice in her own administrative approach and the programs she established in her own schools. The principal knew that Green, despite its many challenges, would nonetheless be an ideal environment in which to put her theories of freedom into practice.

THE STATE OF EDUCATION IN THE EARLY TWENTY-FIRST CENTURY

Children currently in middle school and high school will be graduating from college into an economy where, it is estimated, in 2025, robots will outwork humans by clocking in 52 percent of the hours worked compared to 48 percent for humans, according to the World Economic Forum.[3] In the 2020s, many industries (e.g., automotive, financial services, supply chain, oil and gas, aerospace, etc.) will be hooked up with artificial intelligence, digitization, and robotic processing automation (RPA). Children in middle school and high school will be graduating from college into this marketplace, where robots will have supplanted 75 million jobs that do not require the specialty of the human brain.

So, what jobs will be left, and what will students need to be able to do? The key ability of the human brain that cannot be digitized or mechanized is its ability to *interpret*—that is, "to cope with" the intentions of another, to understand "what was said" and "what was meant," or to discern what was said and what was not said.[4] Humans have the ability to work together as a team toward a common goal (i.e., cooperate), to be altruistic and make sacrifices to help others, to build trust, and to feel empathy or sympathy—and robots do not.[5] *Schools need to know how to prepare students to develop and leverage these singularly human abilities.*

Educators create and engage in endless binary debates about best schooling practices, including phonics versus balanced literacy; explicit teaching versus constructivist learning; cultural diversity of texts versus the canon; mandates versus consensus leadership; and small schools versus large schools. But most of these problems and their solutions operate outside the learners themselves. The impulse of teachers—who are overworked, under-supported, and overwhelmed—to simply go back to what is familiar, and open their same old teaching manuals, is certainly understandable. However, the need to develop students' critical thinking skills cannot be overstated—and a freedom-oriented approach does just that.

According to the Foundation for Critical Thinking, high school and college students are not effectively taught critical thinking. That failure is making our students less competitive: US schools globally rank just above average in reading and science and below average in math, according to the Program for International Student Assessment and the Organization for Cooperation and Development. Despite all the funding allotted for the US educational system, K–12 schools continue to churn out young people unprepared for the economy of the future. *A freedom-based approach doesn't require more money—which means it is applicable to schools across the economic spectrum.*

HOW HISTORIC FAILURE CAME TO A NEW YORK CITY HIGH SCHOOL

The Urban Assembly School for Green Career's graduation rate in 2013 was a mere 39 percent and had been hovering around that number for several years—even though Green didn't technically exist as a separate, independent school before then. It is worth taking a moment here to explain how Green came to exist in its current incarnation, which will also make clear the greater educational culture surrounding the school.

Shortly after 9/11, in 2002, Michael R. Bloomberg, then the mayor of New York, gained control of the New York City Department of Education; prior to that, the Department had been overseen by the Board of Education. In 2007, Mayor Bloomberg announced a complete restructuring of the school system that gave principals more autonomy over their schools in exchange for full accountability based on their data metrics.

The metrics would be reported in the form of annual school report cards, with grades from A to F. When he announced this initiative, Mayor Bloomberg told principals that these report cards would "hold [their] feet to the fire." The schools would also experience a lengthy internal "Quality Review" process each year.

In 2009, also as part of Mayor Bloomberg's restructuring program, large, underperforming schools were reconfigured and broken up into newer, smaller institutions. Louis D. Brandeis High School, a behemoth with 2,251 students, had experienced a perpetually low graduation rate of 30 percent or lower since at least 2001. The 2001 data table included here shows Louis D.

Brandeis High School with a 39 percent graduation rate in 2001 and astoundingly high dropout and student-discharge rates.[6]

New York broke Louis D. Brandeis High School up into three smaller schools: a screened, college-track high school; a transfer school for students two years behind; and an unscreened school that would prepare students for careers in alternative energy. This last school would become the Urban Assembly School for Green Careers.

THE URBAN ASSEMBLY AND GREEN CAREERS: AN OVERVIEW

Green was the first career/technical education school created by the Urban Assembly, meaning it would provide both a career and a college-tracked education. The Urban Assembly Network consists of twenty-three high-performing small schools that are open to all students in New York City; they serve over nine thousand students from lower-income neighborhoods. Each school is centered around a core theme supported by committed partnerships that help guide the curriculum and the school culture.

When the Urban Assembly for Green Careers opened in 2009, at the apex of the era of school reform led by Mayor Bloomberg and Joel Klein (the chancellor of the NYC Department of Education under Bloomberg), hopes were high that true change would finally come to New York City schools. The Brandeis students who did not get accepted anywhere else would remain at Green Careers.

Final Outcomes (Number of Students) for the Class of 2001
by School and Region

	Number of Students Who:			
School Name	**Graduated**	**Dropped Out**	**Total N**	**Discharged**
A. PHILIP RANDOLPH HIGH SCHOOL	235	20	255	74
BEACON HIGH SCHOOL	132	10	142	23
BRANDEIS YABC	14	25	39	9
BREAD & ROSES INTEGRATED ARTS HS	62	14	76	15
CHOIR ACADEMY OF HARLEM	33	7	40	7
FIORELLO H. LAGUARDIA HIGH SCHOOL	463	18	481	84
FREDERICK DOUGLASS ACADEMY	122	8	130	16
GEORGE WASHINGTON HIGH SCHOOL	116	37	153	41
GREGORIO LUPERON HS FOR SCIENCE AND MATHEMAT	17	25	42	53
LOUIS D. BRANDEIS HIGH SCHOOL	248	204	452	175
MARTIN LUTHER KING JR. HIGH SCHOOL	211	98	309	145
THURGOOD MARSHALL ACADEMY	48	17	65	13
WADLEIGH SCHOOL	64	12	76	16
REGION 10	**1766**	**498**	**2264**	**671**

Figure 1.1. Final Outcomes (Number of Students) for the Class of 2001 by School and Region

Since the mission of the Urban Assembly School for Green Careers' is to be an unscreened high school that takes all students, most of the students who would have enrolled at Louis D. Brandeis High School, along with students from other schools around New York City who did not get accepted into any of their top choices, came to Green Careers. The Urban Assembly School for Green Careers, simply put, accepted the students that no other school did.

However, the unintended result of this altruism on the part of Green was that, technically, not a single student actually wanted to go there. Green was not any parent's or child's first choice.

Despite these inauspicious origins, the first and founding principal of Green did some excellent work. Under her stewardship, the school secured excellent partnerships, including the Central Park Conservancy, Friends of Roosevelt Island, the Association for Energy Affordability, and the Manhattan Chamber of Commerce, which ensured students and teachers had access to more opportunities such as internships, curriculum support, and mentoring.

She searched across the globe for promising practices to bring to the school. From methods learned in Singapore, to programming six-week, project-based learning courses on single subjects, this passionate and visionary founding principal experimented with many methods to see what might work for these kids, who were in the bottom 1 percent of New York City school students.[7]

Despite her heroic efforts, by 2013, The Urban Assembly School for Green Careers had failed to attain its goal of reaching a higher graduation rate than the old Brandeis High School it had replaced. Four years after opening Green's doors, it looked as if creating a small school out of a monolithic one was not particularly helpful or successful. Green still rated in the bottom 1 percent of New York City schools, with a 39 percent graduation rate and an "F" on the School Progress Report of 2012–2013.

Around this time, the school suffered a mass exodus of staff and students. However, not all hope was lost, because a small group of talented and committed teachers and one administrator remained, and they clung to their belief that at least one of their innovative methods, if only given the full support it needed, might actually work. These teachers wrote a moving letter to The Urban Assembly:

> We are afraid the danger is that unless a new leader is able to come in before the end of the year and coalesce a core community of staff around a clear, consistent vision, most staff will transfer to a school which is able to offer them this. . . . Ideally, this leader could also have frank conversations with staff members to get a commitment to stay or ascertain if they really are leaving (most people we've spoken to are very open about their preference). If this isn't possible, we're afraid many strong teachers will leave or, at the least, feel disempowered going into September.

The Urban Assembly knew that the teachers who wrote this letter were the strongest teachers in the school and that they were committed to staying if the right principal was brought in to lead and support them. Upon receiving this letter, they thought of the New York City principal who had previously experimented with a freedom-based pedagogy in another school, with proven results.

THE PHONE RANG: "I NEED A JOE CLARK."

When the principal, Kerry Decker Rutishauser, answered the phone call in 2013 asking her to take over a struggling New York City high school, she knew the school was failing—but she did not know how deeply and historically ingrained this failure was.

The person on the other end of the phone didn't waste any time. "I need you to take Green Careers. We need a Joe Clark to take over the school." The principal laughed because she knew what that meant. The school was having a "Joe Clark moment"—referring to the turnaround principal in Paterson, New Jersey, made famous by the movie *Lean On Me*. Clark was an authoritarian leader who believed in strict discipline. Clark had famously said, "If there is no discipline, there is anarchy. Good citizenship demands attention to responsibilities as well as rights."

The principal completely agreed—her belief in and devotion to student freedom did not mean that she rejected discipline. Rather, she believed both were absolutely necessary to a successful, innovative school. This principal wanted nothing more than to take over a perpetually failing school, to prove that a pedagogy of freedom based on student intentionality and self-control can turn around an already failed school.

Without a moment of hesitation, she said, "I am honored you thought of me—I'll take it." But—she was pregnant, and so she needed to have her baby first. Moreover, she had been looking forward to spending some time at home with her infant. "So, how is this going to work?" she asked. He told her, "Invite the teachers up to your house this summer. They will be really excited you are going to be the principal."

This important get-together between the new principal and the teachers is discussed in-depth in the next chapter—but first, how had this incoming principal developed and honed her educational approach?

THEORY THAT MATTERS: EMPOWERING TEACHERS AND STUDENTS

The high-stakes, high-accountability environment of No Child Left Behind, and the highly bureaucratic nature of schooling (even in charter and private schools), stifles and impedes innovation and experimentation. Educators rarely experiment with revolutionary ideas based on theory. Scholars and scientists do their research and write their books—which few teachers or principals read. Who has time to read theory, when all that really matters is how well students perform on the April exams?

Many people just want to be told what to do step-by-step and don't have time to get into the questions of *why* we teach like we teach. Many teachers don't trust that those academics, sitting comfortably in their ivory towers, have any clue of what it is really like in the trenches. What people too often perceive as innovative or progressive practices are merely slightly changed versions of the same old oppressive teaching practices.

RETHINKING WRITING AND READING, EMBRACING FREEDOM

It was 2006, and the principal was observing a second-grade class at her school, Jacob Riis, on the Lower East Side of Manhattan. The kids were on a colorful rug facing the teacher, who was comfortably seated in her rocking chair and pointing to her big book and a pad of chart paper on the easel. The principal waited for the succinct teaching point—that is, the brief, to-the-point "takeaway" strategy that the teacher hopes to impart, which the students will continue to work on in their independent work time—but fifteen minutes passed, and still no teaching point had arrived.

She jotted down everything the teacher said in the left-hand column on her legal pad and everything the students said in the right-hand column. Fifteen minutes and counting, and the left column was still filled with teacher talk, and the right column was empty. The kids sat passively, silently, and dutifully, looking at the teacher—which, to be fair, was a huge feat in and of itself on the part of the teacher, in any conventional educational setting. But even though the kids were respectful and mostly attentive, the principal couldn't help but think, "Something is so very wrong with this."

She had thought all along that she was working in a progressive school: After all, kids were reading and writing every day and there were no teacher-directed worksheets here! Who was she, a thirty-year-old neophyte principal raised in Wisconsin, to question these East Coast, big city, Ivy League-trained, published gurus and their models, as well as the teachers who followed them? Even so, once she started to observe this insidious silence and stillness on the part of students, she knew she had a big problem.

That day, she left that second-grade class without finishing the observation, vowing to change these oppressive rug practices immediately. She realized the silencing of student voices carried over into everything else teachers were doing. Into the quiet hallways, she roamed, once again avoiding the student-authored narratives on the walls because, as cute as they were, she was going to die of boredom reading them.

The writing lacked genuine purpose, voice, and creativity. Why do children in grades K–8 always have to write in the narrative genre at the beginning of each or at the same time of the year? Why can't kids be more intentional and write on topics of their own interest, in the genres of their own choosing? Heck, why can't kids write more together, in small groups? Why can't writing be a creative, self-directed, interpersonal activity? Indeed, why can't kids work together in all of their classes and in all of their schoolwork?

She realized that, despite her school's seemingly innovative practices, they were still basically using the same old traditional, and even oppressive, teaching practices. She also realized that, despite their supposedly creative and engaging approaches to literacy, kids in the school still disliked reading, to the point where many children shied away from any and all text. Some kids went through the motions of reading, but they definitely were not having fun, whether reading independently or with others.

She worked after school with a group of students who were perpetually stuck in the lower-level reading groups. She wanted to figure out what would inspire them to actually want to read. What she found out was that they just plain disliked all texts and refused to read anything. Students would do just about anything to avoid looking at a written text. At this school, children could choose which books they wanted to read, but the word "choice" deceived students into thinking that they had an absolute and total choice.

In reality, student book choice was limited to a few options from a leveled library. Students couldn't necessarily pick books based on their own interests, because they were confined to their own assessed-reading, leveled-text choices, which they found in leveled boxes or bins—and students couldn't move out of their level until the teacher got around to assessing each student again!

THE LITERACY EPIPHANY

Literacy is stringing letters and sounds together, learning the precise meaning of words, and gaining content knowledge—and it is so much more! It's not just about sitting around a kidney-shaped table or in a round-robin reading group with a teacher who directs students in their reading and writing. Putting students in leveled groups restricts a student's text choice, it restricts a student's access to a diversity of ideas and complex literature, and it limits oral discourse patterns.

In leveled-reading groups, students generally learn only what the teacher directs them to know. This approach to the teaching of reading reduces a child's literacy activity down to a reading strategy, or a vocabulary or grammar lesson, with no time left for engaging in cooperative (and creative) thought and shared discourse.

Child psychologist and author David R. Olson asserts that literacy is about knowing how to be part of the discourse of a textual community, in which people can interpret, hypothesize, infer, and deduce based on a shared text. People who are literate know how to choose texts because they know which ones are important and relevant to their needs and wishes at that moment in time. A literate person knows how to think about what the author intended the words to mean and can apply these thoughts to their own speech and actions.[8]

Along these same lines, the United Nations Educational, Scientific and Cultural Organization (UNESCO) defines literacy as the "ability to identify, understand, interpret, create, communicate and compute, using printed and written materials associated with varying contexts. Literacy involves a continuum of learning in enabling individuals to achieve their goals, to develop their knowledge and potential, and to participate fully in their community and wider society."

Literate people, therefore, strengthen their literacy skills by engaging in literate talk and thinking activity within and outside their immediate community (in this case, school). Literacy must mean, then, the ability to flexibly navigate a wide range of social groups and ideas, choose texts, make queries and set goals, pursue independent thinking, engage in conversation and debate with all kinds of thinkers and readers, predict and debate an author's intentions and a reader's response, read and think beyond a particular reading "level," and challenge personal ideas in relation to those held by others.

Olson notes that very young children acquire the "concepts of relevance to literate thinking—think, know, mean, might be, could be, must be" through "ordinary oral discourse."[9] There are no limits to literacy improvement if students have open access to other minds and texts and can talk to each other. Why, then, do we impose so many limits on reading—and so much else—in schools?

THE READING COLOR LINE: SEGREGATION BEGINS IN KINDERGARTEN

After more than a year of conducting meetings and visiting classrooms, this young principal started to notice that kids stayed mostly in static, homogenous, leveled reading groups all year long. This Lower East Side school was truly a diverse school: The population in grade 6–8 broke down roughly as 25 percent Asian, 25 percent black, 25 percent Latino, and 25 percent white. She couldn't help but notice how the color line began to form across the whole school as a result of leveled reading programs that started in kindergarten.

The black and brown kids noticed this and talked and wrote about it too, often referring to the honors-level reading and math classes as "the place where the white kids from Tribeca [a wealthy neighborhood in Manhattan's financial district] go to class." She began to argue that leveling students in reading groups is a segregationist practice: It not only restricts student access to literate concepts, oral discourse, and thought, it also creates a color line in the school. The final straw came when she entered a kindergarten classroom for another day of observation. She had just ordered a ton of big books for the classrooms, and she was expecting to see kids lying all over them during center time, looking at the pictures, laughing, and maybe sounding out the letters or words together or independently.

When she walked in, she saw one big book in the hands of the teacher and a few on the easel, but not one of the new books that she had ordered were in the hands of the kids. When she asked the teacher where the rest of the books were, the teacher told her, "They are in the closet."

"Why?" the principal asked.

"The kids are not ready for them yet."

This was perplexing. "What do you mean they are not ready for them yet?"

The teacher responded with confidence (and a touch of condescension), "I haven't taught into it yet. I need to introduce the book to them first and preview the vocabulary words."

The principal wanted to scream, "What? Really? What about the pictures? What if the students huddle around this book and play with the sounds in words and pictures, and while doing so, one of the students identifies a word, reads it out loud, and now the group knows the word they didn't know before that moment? Why can't we increase the chances of maybe one kid pulling everyone up around him by giving kids access to these books before you *teach into it*?" The principal told the teacher to open the closet and get out all the big books—by tomorrow—to liberate the students *and* the teacher!

At that moment, the principal decided that she needed to implement a pedagogy that gave kids and teachers more autonomy and voice and that would be supported by resources that helped students to be agents of their own learning in a social setting. She was going to start a pedagogy of freedom. She searched for a scholar who could help her achieve her vision of giving students more autonomy and voice in the classroom.

Her goal was to develop a theory core so that teachers and administrators could make their own decisions and not be dependent on someone else's version of how curriculum should look in the classroom. After several trials and interviews with scholars and consultants, she hired a literacy professor in education from New York University (NYU). She liked the professor's theory of student intentionality, in which the primary goal of any curriculum is to help students carry out their own intentions. This aligned with the principal's vision of wanting to implement a pedagogy that was more centered on student autonomy and voice in the classroom.

With a literacy professor from NYU as her innovation partner, along with a core group of committed teachers, the principal started to experiment with applying theories of mind, such as the aforementioned student intentionality, as well as shared intentions, into classroom practice.

PUTTING A THEORY CORE INTO PRACTICE: AN ISSUE OF EQUITY

Why was the kindergarten example the final straw? Because access—to information, to resources, to knowledge, to each other's brains, to challenging books—is at the heart of true education. The tight control of information and resources that accompanies these programs, which are marketed as student-centered, is actually the hallmark of oppressive teaching programs: Kids spend their day mostly being directed by the teacher, silent, sitting, doing what the teacher dictated, with a limited and circumscribed supply of resources. Students were still being asked to merely regurgitate approved reading and writing strategies.

If the teachers, who are in charge of the information in the classroom, learned the theories of intentionality, cooperation, theory of mind, and literacy deeply, it would empower them to think for themselves. Teachers could then be empowered to lead the change toward creating a pedagogy of freedom where kids could, for example, write on topics and in genres of their own choosing, or where students could pick challenging books to read based on interest, rather than from a leveled reader, and do so in the company of others.

David R. Olson notes that very young children acquire the "concepts of relevance to literate thinking-think, know, mean, might be, could be, must be" through "ordinary oral discourse."[10] There are no limits to literacy learning if students have open access to other minds and texts and can talk to each other. Why, then, do we impose so many limits on reading—and so much else—in schools?

An established and accepted psychological concept, the theory of mind focuses on a person's ability to make their mental states conscious to others. Theory of mind is when someone's inner thoughts, beliefs, and desires are made conscious and then become a metarepresentational object of attention to which others can respond with responses such as, "this is false."[11]

Teachers are failing to acknowledge the relevance and influence of theory of mind when they say things such as "make your thinking visible." Typically, the explicit manifestation of a student's mental state exists in isolation in schools, in the form of a worksheet or a quiz. In exercises like these, students are not making their own genuine thinking visible. Rather, they are making visible the thinking that the teacher either wants them or allows them to make. When assignments, text choice, and options for collaboration are teacher driven, the student's output is just a response, without any authentic thought involved or encouraged.

This is where equity is an issue: Kids who don't understand the thinking the teacher is asking for suffer, as do those students who stifle their own voices for the sake of a right answer and a good grade. This isolated form of "making your thinking visible" exists in a vacuum, and it totally eliminates the opportunities for any authentic and immediate social response in the moment, where change and learning are most likely to occur. Helping students learn to share their inner thoughts with other students, who are then free to respond in the moment, would be a fundamental move toward giving students more autonomy, voice, and freedom in the classroom.

THEORY OF MIND IN PRACTICE: CREATING A WINDOW TO SEE WHAT IS POSSIBLE AND VALUED

One example of several theory of mind practices that the principal implemented successfully at the school on the Lower East Side of Manhattan, and which she mandated across the school, was called Cooperative Unison Reading® (several examples of this practice in action appear throughout the book, including an earlier one in the Introduction).[12] To show the staff what is valued and possible and prove to herself and to the kids that this method was going to be a viable solution to low achievement in reading, the principal taught it with the lowest baseline of students in the school.

This was a group of special needs adolescent boys from a 12:1:1 class, meaning that they need a restrictive classroom with only twelve students like themselves in it, one teacher, and one paraprofessional. The boys in the group carried many labels to signify their special needs. All of them were at least two or more years below grade level in terms of academic skills. Some were severely emotionally disturbed, learning disabled, speech delayed, or a combination of these issues. Nobody at the school wanted to teach this group.

Here is an example of what some of the lowest baseline of kids can do if the adults show them how to cooperate and then move out of their way. Read here how they grapple with the meaning of what the author said and what the author meant in the text and the "say-mean"[13] distinction fundamental to people's interpretation of what things mean on the written page.

Students read out loud and in sync a text they had chosen about football. The students across the school would choose short articles from the plethora of magazine titles (such as *TIME for Kids*, *National Geographic*, *Kids Discover*, and *Ranger Rick*) that the school ordered for every classroom in the school. Students could choose an article to read, changing articles and groups every two weeks.

Anthony: Oh, you bum. I don't want to read this no more. He's wack. In two seasons? You get way more than that!

Jacob: Not really, that's good! That's a good amount.

A: Yes, I would. Fifty touchdowns!?

Elon: He already scored like one hundred.

J: That's good for a running back.

A: Two seasons?

J: It's not about being tall.

Daniel: Wait, I still don't know what you mean by two seasons?

Principal: You want to check in with Daniel, he had a question.

E: What's the question?

D: I need help with the meaning of "two seasons."

A: Two seasons is when . . . look, basketball is one year.

D: Is it different from the winter and spring? It's different, right?

A: It doesn't matter the season. It can go whenever. A season is when you start playing a sport all the way to the end of the sport. And two seasons is when you do it twice.

E: Now do you get it?

D: Yeah.

They read again out loud and in sync.

D: Stop.

E: What do "gridiron" mean? (pronouncing it incorrectly)

J: (corrects Elon and sounds it out correctly) *Grid-i-ron.* A field. That means.

E: Like the movie?

J: Yea, like the movie.

Principal: Does everyone have it?

E: Yes, we have it. It's a football field, like the gridiron games.

Principal: As a leader, you have to decide if you are all ready to move on or if you need to talk about it some more.

E: We are ready to move on.

In this small amount of time (only five minutes), a group of special-needs adolescent boys figured out what was communicated in a text and what the author meant to say (i.e., say-mean), and how what was said could be applied to their own lives! The process to get them to read together in sync and stop and talk to each other took a lot of work on the part of the principal, but once they started to follow the rules of the cooperative process, the only thing she did was remind the group leader to make sure the group heard Daniel, and that they all came to a common understanding about what "two seasons" and "gridiron" meant before moving on.

They took responsibility for their own learning. They chose their own text about football. They could stop whenever they needed to ask a question about words they didn't know how to pronounce or what a word meant (such as "gridiron" and "two seasons") or concepts they didn't get ("It's not about being tall") and talk about it. The students even decided when it was time to move on from a conversation about what things meant on the page and read together again. Their minds stayed in sync.

If students could spend most of their school time like this, trying to figure out what the author meant to say from texts that students chose to read in the company of others, we would not have a critical thinking crisis in our country today.

The principal worked with the middle school boys every day, to the point where she was able to begin integrating them into the mainstream classrooms. Her efforts resulted in noticeable, statistically significant achievement gains across subgroups in the school, and this caused people to take notice.[14]

One day, in 2009, when the principal was working with her 12:1:1 boys, who were totally engaged in their reading together, a new teacher at the time,

Madeleine "Maddie" Ciliotta-Young, watched in amazement as this principal put the new innovation into practice with the hardest-to-reach students. Word had gotten out about what this principal was able to do with this 12:1:1 special education class, so Maddie came to visit and watch them work. She still has her notes from that visit, which included the phrase, "Unison Reading!!!!" written in bold and circled many times.

Fast-forward four years after Maddie watched the principal in the 12:1:1 class. It was 2013, and The Urban Assembly School for Green Careers was now a school in crisis. And this brings the narrative back to when the principal's phone rang, when Maddie, along with a core group of teachers, asked her to be the principal to implement this pedagogy of freedom across their entire high school—and save it from extinction.

NOTES

1. Cynthia McCallister, *Unison Reading: Social Inclusive Group Instruction for Equity and Achievement* (New York: Corwin Press, 2011).
2. Ibid.
3. World Economic Forum, "The Future of Jobs Report 2018," September 17, 2018, https://www.weforum.org/reports/the-future-of-jobs-report-2018.
4. David R. Olson, *The World On Paper: The Conceptual and Cognitive Implications of Writing and Reading* (Cambridge, UK: Cambridge University Press, 1994), 93, 128–30.
5. Michael Tomasello, *Becoming Human: A Theory of Ontogeny* (Cambridge, MA and London, England: Harvard University Press, 2019).
6. New York City Department of Education of Assessment and Accountability. *The Class of 2001 Final Longitudinal Report: A Three-Year Follow-UP Study 2005 Report.*
7. New York City Department of Education, "Progress Report 2012–13," http://schools.nyc.gov/Accountability/tools/accountability/default.htm.
8. Olson, *The World On Paper*, 273–82.
9. Olson, *The World on Paper*, 281.
10. Olson, *The World on Paper*, 281.
11. David R. Olson, *The Mind on Paper: Reading, Consciousness and Rationality* (Cambridge, UK: Cambridge University Press, 2016), 77–79.
12. McCallister, *Unison Reading.*
13. Olson, *The World On Paper*, 130.
14. McCallister, *Unison Reading*, 93–106.

Chapter Two

The Principles of Freedom

The principal's first day at Green was immediately challenging—perhaps to be expected in a school where just ten percent of incoming freshmen had passed the statewide, eighth-grade English Language Arts exam. Before classes had even begun, she was made aware of a student, Esteban, who had come to school with the smell of alcohol on his breath. The principal's extensive interactions with Esteban, discussed in this chapter, show how the pedagogical theories being proposed actually look in practice, on the ground, with demanding and challenging kids. Although the principal suspended Esteban, he returned to school the very next day, this time wearing an extremely inappropriate T-shirt depicting a nude woman, marijuana leaves, and guns. Esteban insisted that he could wear whatever clothing he wished.

The principal, rather than scolding or arguing, agreed with Esteban. He did have that right—but, she pointed out, other students, especially younger ones, might find the shirt frightening or threatening, and as a member of the school community, and one of the older students, he had a responsibility to think about the message his clothing sent. The principal continued this line of conversation by encouraging Esteban to describe his other T-shirts and to perhaps choose another one to wear instead. She also took a moment to pause and self-interrogate, thinking aloud about whether or not Esteban actually was breaking any rules by wearing the graphic T-shirt, and then suggesting that they consult the Blue Book (the NYC Department of Education rules and guidelines) together. Throughout this exchange, the principal does not shut down conversation, encourages the student to think about self-responsibility and the ramifications of his actions, and presents herself as someone who can second-guess herself—a partner, rather than an all-knowing disciplinarian.

This process does not always unfold smoothly, as students often throw up roadblocks of resistance. For example, Esteban insisted that, given his ADHD diagnosis, he couldn't change his behaviors. The principal responded that such a diagnosis, while useful, did not render him helpless or hopeless: "If you say you want to change, you can and will, and we will help you." In another tricky moment, the principal asked Esteban if he wanted to change his behav-

ior, to which he honestly replied, "I'm not sure. I think I like it this way." Rather than protest, or dismiss this answer, the principal accepted it, noting that it was a fair response, as his behaviors have earned him a position as a "negative leader" at the school. To help Esteban transition toward being a positive leader, the principal helped him write down all of the behaviors he wanted to change and elicited a verbal promise from him to change.

The interaction with Esteban illustrates and introduces the Five Principles of Freedom: Think (guide students to practice self-control and consider the ramifications of their actions); Build (encourage a sense of community by soliciting verbal and written pledges and promises to enact and model right behaviors); Act (show students how to act with intention, by listing and considering their own behaviors); Speak (allow students to speak honestly, without preaching at, dismissing, or lecturing them); and Fight (help students understand that freedom must be valued, protected, and fought for, and that by becoming positive leaders, they can preserve this freedom for others). The Principles of Freedom can be applied to help students build their own positive academic and behavioral change narratives.

FIRST DAY, FIRST THEORIES—IN PRACTICE

From day one, the staff were clear-eyed about the challenges awaiting them at Green.

Many of the students were from some of the poorest zip codes not only in New York but in the entire United States. The majority of students read six to seven years *below* grade level. That's right: Most students read at a mere second to third grade reading level as measured on the 2013 Degrees of Reading Power Exam, a nationally norm-referenced reading comprehension test.

Perhaps to be expected given these conditions, the principal's on-the-ground experience at Green was less than encouraging on day one. That first morning, not long after classes had started, the principal exited her second-floor office to use the bathroom only to hear a girl screaming at the top of her lungs down the hallway, "Suck my dick!"

So instead of going to the bathroom, the principal walked in front of this student to get her attention, before the student could run off down the stairwell. When the principal stepped into the girl's view, she turned to the principal, put the palm of her hand one inch in front of the principal's face, said, "Shut up, bitch" (even though the principal hadn't said anything), and ran off.

And with that, the principal had her first interaction with a student at Green.

Even students who were actually attending classes were not much better. Students were shopping for shoes on Amazon during class, watching hip-hop videos on YouTube, playing violent video games, ordering lunch delivery, attending their friends' classes, calling Uber to pick them up to get pizza in Harlem, or watching movies on their phones.

The answer to this unacceptable situation was, counterintuitively, more freedom, more autonomy, and more responsibility. As absurd as it might seem, the principal was sure that if she gave students freer rein to act on their own intentionality, a healthier and more productive school environment would be the result.

JUMPING RIGHT INTO THE DEEP END WITH ESTEBAN

Most of the principal's beliefs and practices were put to the test that very first day, by a student named Esteban. This chapter will highlight what theory looks like in practice—and show how it's necessary to constantly refine and adapt any approach on the ground, every day, to meet the students where they are, from day one.

As any principal knows, the first day of school always brings a surprise or two. But because of all the stories that people had told her about Green, this principal set her expectations really low: Her only goal was to be able to greet students at scanning (where the students enter and go through metal detectors and security) in the morning.

Twenty minutes before school started, her phone rang. It was Eli, the community associate: "I have a student, Esteban, down here at the entrance who smells like alcohol. He's been drinking."

A few thoughts quickly ran through the principal's mind. *Do I ask Eli to bring him to the nurse's office, then to his own office to call the student's mother*? No—she decided she would tackle this herself. She lamented the fact that she wouldn't get to meet all of the other students at the front door on the first day of school.

She took a second to think and responded, "Eli, take him to the nurse to make sure he is OK. Call his mother to come to my office. Bring Esteban to me as soon as he is done at the nurse. You come too."

She went to the bathroom, and by the time she came back, Eli and Esteban were waiting in her office. Esteban's mother arrived soon after. The principal began first and asked Esteban, "Why are you drinking before school? Were you nervous about the first day of school?"

Esteban said, "No, but sometimes I take a few drinks or smoke a little before school starts. It calms me down and helps me deal with all the annoying shit that happens here."

The principal and Eli talked to Esteban about why he would feel the need to drink before school in order to deal with the "annoying shit." Was he anxious? Was he doing other drugs besides smoking marijuana?

With an openness you don't always see in teenagers, Esteban told everyone, "Like cocaine? No, no. No hard drugs. Just alcohol and weed."

The principal decided, "You need to go home with your mom today. This is a suspension. Let this experience be the thing you think about the next time you want to drink or smoke before school starts."

His mother nodded her head in agreement. The two sat close to each other, and when the principal broke the news, Esteban put his hand on her arm to reassure her that things would be OK. Esteban and his mom were close—us-against-the-world close. Everyone shook hands and hugged each other. When Esteban and his mother left, the principal looked at Eli and thought, *This school is a piece of cake!*

The next day, walking toward the cafeteria, who did the principal see in the hallway but Esteban, wearing a T-shirt emblazoned with a picture of a naked woman sitting on top of two giant marijuana leaves and holding a gun in each hand. When she called out Esteban's name and tried to get his attention, he looked at her and then walked away.

Still not sure how to use it, she clumsily contacted Eli on her walkie-talkie. She asked Eli to find Esteban, if he could, and bring him to her office. Within minutes, Eli showed up in her office with Esteban trailing behind him. This was a good sign; it showed that Esteban wanted to engage with her because he could have walked out of school, but instead, he let himself be found. As she prepared to speak, he snapped, "I can wear what I want at school. This T-shirt is not going to hurt anyone."

The principal could have chosen to assert, declare, or scold—but she chose to agree with him. "That's true. You can wear this T-shirt, and it's not going to hurt anyone. But it could scare people, especially young children. There are little kids in this building. Kids of all ages walk in our hallways because our school sits in the middle of all the other schools. Don't you see the charter school elementary kids marching around like little soldiers everywhere?"

He laughed. The students and staff at Green all instinctively disliked the charter school in the building. No one liked how the charter-school teachers spoke to the kids, or how they treated the kids like robots.

The principal continued, "When I tried to stop you, you were right outside the daycare facility's door. You chose to wear a shirt depicting a naked lady sitting on two pot leaves holding two guns, a day after I suspended you, and a day after I spent two hours getting to know you and your mother in my office on the first day of school. What does that tell you about me and how I feel about you? I could have spent my time a hundred different ways as the new principal on the first day of school, but I spent most of my day with you and your mom, tucked away inside my office, Esteban."

Esteban cut to the chase in his reply: "Are you scared of my T-shirt?"

She replied, "No, I'm not scared of a T-shirt. I am all about free expression, and maybe you'll learn to trust me on that later, but for right now, I think that you have a responsibility to show leadership and make sure other students feel comfortable around you. At Green, you have to sit together, talk together, and look at each other to learn. This T-shirt can send the wrong message to others about your intentions, and some people may not feel safe with you in the room. I do think this is a violent looking T-shirt that sends a violent and confusing message out into the school."

He responded, "How do you know other kids will care what I wear or what it says? Who cares about my T-shirt?"

Encouraged by this response, the principal asked him, "What other T-shirts do you have that you can wear that tells people more about you?" He let it all out on the table. He proudly told them both about his T-shirt collection. He had all kinds, from SpongeBob to guns to drugs, and he continued to argue, "So, why can't I wear the naked-lady marijuana leaf with guns T-shirt then? It's not going to scare anyone."

"Yes," the principal replied, "but people might mistake you for a drug dealer in the school. Again, what would be your intention for wearing a T-shirt of a marijuana leaf, with a naked woman holding two guns pointed at the viewer to school? It could also possibly make kids feel uncomfortable around you in the classroom. What will it teach the younger kids?"

Undeterred, Esteban continued, "I have a T-shirt with just a naked woman. It's really awesome." He started to describe it in greater detail—but the principal promptly cut him off. In response, he began explaining that all his T-shirts expressed his personality, and he chose which one to wear each day, depending on his feelings that morning.

The principal asked lightheartedly, "What is wrong with wearing the SpongeBob T-shirt? Can't you just wear SpongeBob tomorrow? Then I won't have to stop to talk to you about your T-shirt in the hallway, and you won't feel the need to walk away and ignore me. I think you need to decide if you want to be a negative or positive leader at this school."

But then it occurred to her that Esteban might be right. Why couldn't he wear these T-shirts?

"Actually, wait," she said. "You actually might be right, Esteban. Maybe you can wear this marijuana-leaf, naked-lady-with-guns T-shirt, and maybe I am in the wrong. I just think it sends out a negative leadership message to others and creates a negative vibe, but let's look at the Blue Book to see if there is anything in there that can guide us." She let the student see her second-guessing herself, interrogating her assumptions, and then turning to an outside source of information and guidance.

Like many students, Esteban didn't even know that he had rights and responsibilities, so they read them out loud together on pages 15 and 16 (see figures 2.1 and 2.2) of the New York Department of Education's *Citywide*

Behavioral Expectations to Support Student Learning (a book with a blue cover, hence "the Blue Book").

BILL OF STUDENT RIGHTS AND RESPONSIBILITIES, K-12

PREAMBLE

New York City public schools seek to cultivate a sense of mutual respect among students, parents and staff. City schools also aim to involve students in activities and programs, within and outside the school community, that stress a commitment to civic responsibility and community service. With the cooperation of all members of our school communities, students can reach educational excellence while enjoying a rich learning experience. This document serves as a guide for students as they strive to become productive citizens in a diverse society.

I. THE RIGHT TO A FREE PUBLIC SCHOOL EDUCATION
The right to a free public school education is a basic "student right" guarenteed to all children.
Students have a right to:

1. attend school and receive a free public school education from kindergarten to age 21 or receipt of a high school diploma, whichever comes first, as provided by law; students who have been determined to be English Language Learners are entitled to bilingual education or English as a second language program as provided by law; students with disabilities who have been determined to be in need of special education are entitled to a free appropriate public education from age 3 until age 21, as provided by law;
2. be in a safe and supportive learning environment, free from discrimination, harassment, bullying, and bigotry, and to file a complaint if they feel that they are subject to this behavior (see Chancellor's Regulations A-830, A-831, A-832, A-420, and A-421);
3. receive courtesy and respect from others regardless of actual or perceived age, race, creed, color, gender, gender identity, gender expression, religion, national origin, citizenship/immigration status, weight, sexual orientation, physical and/or emotional condition, disability, marital status and political beliefs;
4. receive a written copy of the school's policies and procedures, including the Discipline Code and the New York City Department of Education Bill of Student Rights and Responsibilities, early in the school year or upon admission to the school during the school year;
5. be informed about diploma requirements, including courses and examinations and information on assistance to meet those requirements;
6. be informed about required health, cognitive and language screening examinations;
7. be informed about courses and programs that are available in the school and the opportunity to have input in the selection of elective courses;
8. receive professional instruction;
9. know the grading criteria for each subject area and/or course offered by the school and to receive grades for school work completed based on established criteria;
10. be informed of educational progress and receive periodic evaluations both informally and through formal progress reports;
11. be notified in a timely manner of the possibility of being held over in the grade or of failing a course;
12. be notified of the right of appeal regarding holdover or failing grades;
13. confidentiality in the handling of student records maintained by the school system;
14. request or by parental request to have their contact information withheld from institutions of higher learning and/or military recruiters;
15. receive guidance, counseling and advice for personal, social, educational, career and vocational development.

Figure 2.1. Bill of Students Rights and Responsibilities K–12

"DO YOU TELL A TEACHER TO 'SHUT THE FUCK UP' OR 'SUCK MY DICK'?"

This is important: It's vital that students vocalize all of their maladaptive behaviors and the relevant coping mechanisms that hinder their responsibilities and performance in school and then also count out how many of their duties and responsibilities their own behaviors undercut.

So, the principal said, "Esteban, let's list out the behaviors that are getting in the way of your right to learn or the rights of others to learn. Or, if it helps, let's list out the behaviors that might be getting in the way of you getting along with others or even just being a happy person. Just, let's list them out, this is a no-judgment, no-punishment zone. Put it all out on the table so we can figure out how to help you help yourself change them."

Granted, students often resist doing this. They'll literally tie their hoodie up to hide their face, run out of the office, climb under the table, argue, or

II. THE RIGHT TO FREEDOM OF EXPRESSION AND PERSON

All students are guaranteed the right to express opinions, support causes, organize and assemble to discuss issues and demonstrate peacefully and responsibly in support of them, in accordance with policies and procedures established by the New York City Department of Education. **Students have the right to:**

1. organize, promote and participate in a representative form of student government;
2. organize, promote and participate in student organizations, social and educational clubs or teams and political, religious, and philosophical groups consistent with the requirements of the Equal Access Act;
3. representation on appropriate schoolwide committees that influence the educational process, with voting rights where applicable;
4. publish school newspapers and school newsletters reflecting the life of the school and expressing student concerns and points of view consistent with responsible journalistic methods and subject to reasonable regulations based on legitimate pedagogical concerns;
5. circulate, including through electronic circulation, newspapers, literature or political leaflets on school property, subject to reasonable guidelines established by the school regarding time, place and manner of distribution, except where such material is libelous, obscene, commercial or materially disrupts the school, causes substantial disorder or invades the rights of others;
6. wear political or other types of buttons, badges or armbands, except where such material is libelous, obscene or materially disrupts the school, causes substantial disorder or invades the rights of others;
7. post bulletin board notices within the school or on the school website subject to reasonable guidelines established by the school, except where such notices are libelous, obscene, commercial or materially disrupt the school, cause substantial disorder or invade the rights of others;
8. determine their own dress within the parameters of the Department of Education policy on school uniforms and consistent with religious expression, except where such dress is dangerous or interferes with the learning and teaching process;
9. be secure in their persons and belongings and to carry in the school building personal possessions which are appropriate for use on the premises;
10. be free from unreasonable or indiscriminate searches, including body searches;
11. be free from corporal punishment and verbal abuse (as per Chancellor's Regulations A-420 and A-421);
12. decline to participate in the Pledge of Allegiance or stand for the pledge.

III. THE RIGHT TO DUE PROCESS

Every student has the right to be treated fairly in accordance with the rights set forth in this document. **Students have the right to:**

1. be provided with the Discipline Code and rules and regulations of the school;
2. know what is appropriate behavior and what behaviors may result in disciplinary actions;
3. be counseled by members of the professional staff in matters related to their behavior as it affects their education and welfare in the school;
4. know possible dispositions and outcomes for specific offenses;
5. due process with respect to disciplinary action for alleged violations of school regulations for which they may be suspended or removed from class by their teachers; students with disabilities, 504 plans, or who are "presumed to have a disability" have the right to certain protections under IDEA.
6. know the procedures for appealing the actions and decisions of school officials with respect to their rights and responsibilities as set forth in this document;
7. be accompanied by a parent and/or representative at conferences and hearings;
8. the presence of school staff in situations where there may be police involvement.

Figure 2.2. Bill of Students Rights and Responsibilities K–12

simply refuse. But Esteban jumped right in by saying, "Let's see. Well, I'm not afraid to say things to teachers."

"What do you say to teachers?"

He looked up at the principal and paused, suddenly uncertain of how to proceed. Most students, even students as candid as Esteban, typically will not admit what they say until the teacher or principal verbalizes their own words back to them first, which always comes as a shock to kids.

The principal calmly said, "Do you ever tell a teacher to 'shut the fuck up' or 'suck my dick'?"

He laughed, so she smiled and continued, chuckling as she spoke, "See how shocking it sounds to you, those words coming from me? Imagine how the teacher feels when you say it to them in class."

"Everyone says it."

"Even so, should I put that down, that you say those things in class?"

"Yes."

"How should I write it?"

"I tell a teacher to shut the fuck up when I get angry."

"But, when do you get angry? Be specific here."

"I get angry when teachers try to get smart."

"What does that mean? Like when they tell you to stop talking in the mini-lesson?"

"Yes."

"When else? What are you doing when they 'get smart'?"

Esteban said, "So, should we write, I say 'shut the fuck up' to teachers when they tell me to stop talking in the mini-lesson?"

"OK, yes," the principal replied, and then looked at him. "Say it to me then in your own words, because your words matter."

"I tell teachers to shut the fuck up when they get smart with me."

"But, where does this happen the most?"

"In the lesson, if I come to class for the lesson. I usually skip the lesson and come to class fifteen minutes late, especially in Mr. Roberto's classes."

FROM AGENCY TO SELF-CONTROL

Their conversation continued to get into the nitty-gritty details of exactly what Esteban had said. This type of process allows students to become more conscious of where, when, and why their poor behaviors occur. Esteban admitted to many poor and disruptive behaviors: "I wear T-shirts with swear words or drugs on it, I come to classes late if I don't like the topic of the mini-lesson, I come back late from lunch, I curse at teachers, I ignore the principal in the hallways, I leave at lunch, or I come to school after lunch."

After he listed about fifteen behaviors and made sure to write them down in his own words, she then asked him to read the Student Responsibilities on page 18 of the Blue Book (see figure 2.3) and said, "List out how many responsibilities your behaviors get in the way of." This important step helps Esteban begin to transition from a state of mere agency to a state of self-control: As David Olson notes, "Self-control is knowing how to do something. You know what the rule is, and you can express it. 'Linguistic compliance' is the ability to grasp an order and comply with it."[1]

After reading all twenty-four responsibilities, Esteban said, "Number 5: 'Behave in a manner that contributes to a safe learning environment and which does not violate other students' right to learn.' Cursing at teachers can fit under that one . . . and Number 10: 'Behave in a polite, truthful, and cooperative manner toward students and school staff' . . . yeah, I don't do that." Esteban continued and counted a total of eight responsibilities that his behavior blocked or undermined.

V. STUDENT RESPONSIBILITIES

Responsible behavior by each student is the only way in which the rights set forth in this document can be preserved. Violation of some of these responsibilities may lead, in accordance with the Discipline Code, to disciplinary measures. Full acceptance of responsibility with the exercise of rights will provide students with greater opportunity to serve themselves and society. **Students have a responsibility to:**

1. attend school regularly and punctually and make every effort to achieve in all areas of their education;
2. be prepared for class with appropriate materials and properly maintain textbooks and other school equipment;
3. follow school regulations regarding entering and leaving the classroom and school building;
4. help maintain a school environment free of weapons, illegal drugs, controlled substances and alcohol;
5. behave in a manner that contributes to a safe learning environment and which does not violate other students' right to learn;
6. share information with school officials regarding matters which may endanger the health and welfare of members of the school community;
7. respect the dignity and equality of others and refrain from conduct which denies or impinges on the rights of others;
8. show respect for school property and respect the property of others, both private and public;
9. be polite, courteous and respectful toward others regardless of actual or perceived age, race, creed, color, gender, gender identity, gender expression, religion, national origin, citizenship/immigration status, weight, sexual orientation, physical and/or emotional condition, disability, marital status and political beliefs, and refrain from making slurs based on these criteria;
10. behave in a polite, truthful and cooperative manner toward students and school staff;
11. promote good human relations and build bridges of understanding among the members of the school community;
12. use non-confrontational methods to resolve conflicts;
13. participate and vote in student government elections;
14. provide positive leadership by making student government a meaningful forum to encourage maximum involvement;
15. work with school staff in developing broad extracurricular programs in order to represent the range of physical, social and cultural interests and needs of students;
16. observe ethical codes of responsible journalism;
17. refrain from obscene and defamatory communication in speech, writing and other modes of expression, including electronic expression, in their interactions with the school community;
18. express themselves in speech, writing and other modes of expression, including electronic expression in a manner which promotes cooperation and does not interfere with the educational process;
19. assemble in a peaceful manner and respect the decision of students who do not wish to participate;
20. bring to school only those personal possessions which are safe and do not interfere with the learning environment;
21. adhere to the guidelines established for dress and activities in the school gymnasium, physical education classes, laboratories and shops;
22. be familiar with the school Discipline Code and abide by school rules and regulations;
23. provide leadership to encourage fellow students to follow established school policies and practices;
24. keep parents informed of school-related matters, including progress in school, social and educational events, and ensure that parents receive communications that are provided by school staff to students for transmittal to their parents.

Figure 2.3. Bill of Students Rights and Responsibilities K–12

"What about the naked-lady-holding-guns-on-marijuana T-shirt?" The principal wanted to close the loop and get Esteban to reflect on the school norms and what brought them together in the first place. "Does that get in the way of your responsibilities?"

"Actually, I totally forgot about that. Let me see. Maybe it could fit under Number 18: 'Express yourself in a manner that promotes cooperation.'"

By this point, the student usually feels relieved and calm. The next step is important. The principal always asks the student to self-reflect: "So, what do you think now? Do you like having these behaviors attached to you? Would you consider these part of the agreed-upon norms for behavior? Like, is saying 'Shut the fuck up' to a teacher a normal behavior?"

"No. These are not normal behaviors. Necessary, though! Sometimes teachers just talk way too much—you know that!" Esteban responded.

"But, Esteban, you are totally being intentional. You can get rid of these behaviors if you choose to. You can change them so that you can follow your responsibilities better." It is vital to insist that students make a verbal commitment to change to others in the group and to have the students verbally state, "I want to change these behaviors," before moving on.

Making a verbal promise out loud to others helps students change their personal narrative. Verbal promises to others encourage students to feel responsible for changing their behaviors and living up to their vows. A public and verbal promise to others in a supportive and helpful community is the most sacred kind of contract.[2]

Esteban replied with a predictable set of excuses for students who, like him, have been labeled: "But, I have had anger issues all my life—I am ADHD."

Well-meaning people stereotype and pathologize children, especially in schools with a high percentage of students with special needs or from low socioeconomic neighborhoods. These categories of stereotypes and pathologies too often lead to students thinking they are broken and can't change, and to the adults around them assuming that children with these labels cannot meet higher expectations of prosocial behavior and advanced academics.[3]

She replied, "Esteban, you can and will be able to change your behavior. It may take you some time, and you might need lots of help. Maybe even more help than others. It doesn't matter, this is not a competition. If you say you want to change, then you will. We will help you do it."

The intent here is absolutely not to dismiss the very concerning and pressing reality of cognitive struggles, and the value and necessity of coping mechanisms and very real medical diagnoses. Rather, it is to highlight that educators, perhaps unwittingly, write poor and minority students off once they receive a diagnosis of ADHD or the like—and students internalize this dismissal.

She asked Esteban, "Do you want to change these behaviors that you carry around with you?"

He replied, "I'm not sure. I think I like it this way."

Rather than dismiss this by saying something, such as "You can't possibly like it this way!," the principal accepted his honest answer but continued and expanded on it by saying, "Yes. You've done well. You are a successful negative leader. Can't you use your same talent and skills that you have to turn into a positive leader and help the school? You can choose like the top two you want to work on first and then go from there."

They finished Esteban's Principal Behavior Intervention together—the principal's first one at Green, on her second day on the job. Esteban promised to change all of his listed behaviors; he really wanted to work on not cursing at teachers, coming to school sober and wearing more appropriate clothing. Esteban took up the better part of the principal's first and second day at Green, but in retrospect, it was a good use of her time.

During the next three years, Esteban almost completely transformed from a negative influence to a positive leader in the school. Many times, Esteban backed up the school norms. For example, no one at Green will ever forget the time he "saved" the school during the Quality Review, the city's internal school-quality rating system. The reviewer entered his writing classroom for a visit and sat down next to Esteban at a table. Esteban didn't have his writing out in front of him.

Thinking fast, he got up and guided the reviewer on a tour of all the other students' writing pieces. With his flamboyant personality (and his speech littered with curse words), he described each writer's piece from memory. He even included his own personal opinion on whether or not each student's piece was succeeding in its intended purpose.

The reviewer was so impressed with the creativity illustrated in this class's writing that she asked for ten writing pieces to take back with her to prove to her committee that Green was doing great things—and the school went on to receive a perfect Quality Review score that year.

THE THEORY BEHIND THE PRACTICE: THE FIVE PRINCIPLES OF FREEDOM

The theoretical origins and the practical classroom applications of each of the Five Principles of Freedom will be explained throughout this book—but you have already seen them all in practice, in the exchange with Esteban on the principal's first days at Green. The Five Principles of Freedom is a theory core made conscious and active. With this book, these Principles can now serve as a practical and theoretical framework for others to use to guide their practices to support discipline, autonomy, responsibility, and freedom of mind as outcomes. In short, the Five Principles of Freedom are:

- **Think**: Teach kids how to balance freedom and self-control. A pedagogy of freedom is about teaching students how to bring their own mental abilities under control.

The principal showed Esteban that he had the freedom to practice self-control and prosocial behaviors by knowing the norms and learning to be more conscious of them, and coupled them with his own thoughts, beliefs, and actions in the moment.

- **Build**: Show kids how to build a culture of "we-ness."[4] By knowing their responsibilities to each other and contracting with other people, students build a tight-knit community.

When Esteban and the principal created this contract, they both wrote it and signed it together. He made a verbal and written promise to change. His relationship with everyone within the school, over the years, would revolve around and build upon how his needs could become his strengths.

- **Speak**: Show students how to liberate their voices. When people's voices are liberated, their thinking is liberated. Language is the medium that creates, supports, and mediates thinking.

When the principal and Eli sat down with Esteban, they didn't preach to him or lecture him about his behavior. They created the space for him to start to think about his own thoughts by getting him to talk about his behaviors, using his own voice and his own words.

- **Act**: Teach students how to act intentionally, by helping them learn to see where and when their actions are within their own control rather than dictated by another. Acting intentionally allows students to learn how to behave with autonomy, control the information, and create their own sense of selfhood.

From the start of this process with the principal and Eli, Esteban acted within his own control by listing, in his own words, all his behaviors that got in the way. He verbalized his own promise and strategies to change. In each successive follow-up meeting, Esteban would continue to be the lead actor and voice in his own transformation process.

- **Fight**: Teach students how to stand up to tyranny. Freedom must be pursued and protected constantly.

The principal knew that, if Esteban could change from a highly successful negative leader to a positive leader, he could use his leadership skills to fight for other student's freedom of mind and voice in school, something she knew he would believe in and want to pursue.

The principal's encounter with Esteban made her even more confident that this failing and underfunded school could be transformed into a safe and academically challenging learning environment without the need for more money or more staff.

The Principles of Freedom empower teachers to trust themselves and their students, administrators to trust that teachers can and will change if they believe in the students—and students to trust that they can make mistakes, yet still develop their voices and their abilities.

The Five Principles provide reliable support as students learn how to act autonomously, responsibly, and with concern for others. The Five Principles are the foundation behind all of the techniques and processes implemented at Green, and they are illustrated and explained in-depth in the chapters to come. For now, here is a summary of what the principal, the teachers, and the students successfully implemented together at Green:

- With the support of an On Call teacher, who monitored the halls and entered classrooms to support fellow teachers when they requested assistance, teachers conducted over 13,500 classroom "behavior conferences" per year, during which they worked with students one-on-one to help them learn how to think and act in the moment inside the classroom, and how to change their own behaviors to bring them in line with their responsibilities.
- The Keepers of the Culture®[5] (KOC class) met with students approximately a thousand times each year to help students create personal transformational narratives called Promise Cards. Many students met more than twenty-five times with the KOC classes over the course of their high school career.
- The Classroom Responsibility Ladder gave students several restorative opportunities to be consciously aware of their behaviors, and whether those behaviors needed to change in order to align with the prosocial group norms.
- The Learning Conferences helped students build their unique personal learning narratives by understanding how to incrementally build off their strengths and go from the known to the unknown when they get stuck. Students came up with new goals based on where their struggles surfaced and created a new self-narrative of how to learn by using their strengths (by first becoming conscious of them), and then making goals based on how best to use those personal strengths.
- The Writing Share gave students an opportunity to share their writing with the rest of the class and ask for responsive feedback. The Writing Share supported student intentionality, created a communal culture, and helped students become critically conscious learners at the school. Students shared their writing in a Writing Share a minimum of ten times a year. Every student took a mandatory writing class all four years in high school.
- Writing Class was as important as math and reading class at Green. Students wrote on topics and in genres of their own choosing for 210 minutes per week and shared all of their drafts with the class for feedback. Many students opted to share their writing in small groups, an opportunity that was offered daily.
- Students breached all day long (that is, reflected consciously on their own thoughts, reflexes, and actions, as well as those of other students) and determined their own teaching points based on what they were thinking about or struggling with that day.

- Kids participated in an interpretive dialogue with others in Cooperative Unison Reading®[6] or Responsibility Teams for fifty minutes in each class every day. Children read a text that they chose, in groups of their choosing, breached at the point of their own "brain" disjuncture and determined their own teaching points and researched the answers to their own questions.

Green is a testament to the efficacy of these tools; tools that become known collectively as Learning Cultures®.[7]

In the chapters to come, this book will show in more detail how change came to Green—and how it can come to any other school, too.

NOTES

1. David R. Olson, "A New Theory of Agency and Responsibility," Learning Cultures, 2014, https://www.youtube.com/watch?v=x5wwt7l8Lmc.
2. "There is a vast gap between being held responsible and accepting responsibility. The cognitive means that children use to get from ascription to avowal, from being held responsible to being responsible, I shall argue, is the linguistic device of quotation, the quoted rule then causing the action. Put another way, the action takes the form that it does because the actor knows the rule, repeats it to him or herself and applies the rule, its application eventually becoming habitual." From David R. Olson, "Self-Ascription of Intention: Responsibility, Obligation and Self-Control," *Synthese* 159 (August 2007): 297–314, http://doi.org/10.1007/s11229-007-9209-2.
3. C. M. Steele and J. Aronson, "Stereotype Threat and the Intellectual Test Performance of African Americans," *Journal of Personality and Social Psychology* 69, no. 5 (1995): 797–811, http://doi.org/10.1037/0022-3514.69.5.797.
4. Michael Tomasello, *Why We Cooperate* (Boston: MIT Press, 2009).
5. Cynthia McCallister, 2018, https://cynthiamccallister.com/.
6. Cynthia McCallister, *Unison Reading: Social Inclusive Group Instruction for Equity and Achievement* (New York: Corwin Press, 2011).
7. McCallister, 2018, https://cynthiamccallister.com/.

Chapter Three

Build

To gain the support of the teaching staff and create a sense of camaraderie, the principal invited the teachers to her house for an informal meeting before the school year began. Sitting poolside in her backyard in August, the principal heard the teachers' concerns and fears. She knew she had to reassure them that a pedagogy of freedom, perhaps counterintuitively, required a culture of discipline, especially self-discipline, because the freedom to cooperate and to think independently can only work in an atmosphere where self-control and thoughtful, prosocial behaviors are enacted by everyone: teachers, administrators, and students.

But the principal also knew that her approach flew in the face of the usual methods, and change is generally resisted at large institutions. By making it clear that the teachers' cooperation was necessary—that, in fact, this change could not happen if it wasn't initiated by them, every day, in their classrooms—the principal gained their support and trust. A meeting like this can go a long way toward building partnerships and allowing teachers to see that their leader has a clear vision and firm plans backed by theory—and that their input and on-the-ground support is vital.

Another crucial aspect of the meeting was the creation or decision to implement key pedagogical tools, including on-call teachers, behavior conferences, circles of freedom, the school-wide Blue Book talk, and classroom responsibility ladders, which, along with tools and formats devised later in the year, came to be known collectively as Learning Cultures®.[1]

Teachers on-call are staff members assigned to a time slot during which they are responsible for walking the hallways to sweep students into classrooms, watch for any disruptive behaviors, and being available to any teacher in any classroom requiring additional support.

In behavior conferences, the teacher helps the student see the impact and ramifications of their actions and behaviors by asking the student to describe what happened and tell their side of the story, determine what rule their behavior broke, how the behavior interfered with their own and others' learning, and how to immediately re-engage in the learning.

Classrooms were designated as Circles of Freedom and, thus, were characterized as places where students could move about, speak with one another, and direct their own learning, while working cooperatively in self-chosen groups.

Teachers and students together would agree upon the school rules that then became the norms to live by school-wide.

Finally, students would help create the school-wide Classroom Responsibility Ladder, which provides guideposts to appropriate behavior via concrete steps. It's important to allow students to discuss the behaviors that should be considered disruptive so that they can see how various behaviors and actions might be interpreted differently by different people, and so that everyone feels a vested interest in having created the prosocial norms, and thus using the Ladder to uphold them.

As the personal accounts from several students and teachers that are shared in this chapter make clear, upholding these prosocial norms can initially be time-consuming and feel unnatural or counterintuitive, but eventually, as students come to understand the value of the agreed-upon prosocial norms, and how their own behaviors impact others, they gain a sense of ownership over the process, which is key to implementing and maintaining a pedagogy of freedom.

PART I: BUILDING A TEACHER LEADERSHIP CULTURE

In 2013, Green was not a safe place, inside or outside. Teachers were spit on, punched, sexually harassed, and threatened by students. Many students came to school just to deal drugs in the hallways. The smell of marijuana emanated from stairwells and bathrooms. Students took over locker rooms to gamble. One student snorted a condom up one nostril and out her mouth in class. And if anyone dared call a student out for any misbehavior, that student would most likely tell that person to "suck my dick."

And yet, despite this chaotic environment, giving students opportunities for self-determination and freedom is what led to Green's turnaround. And, of course, the teachers played a huge role in the development of this new culture of freedom and discipline.

This chapter shows how the principal and teachers together planned to implement radically progressive ideas about discipline, autonomy, and voice—ideas more usually put into practice in private or wealthier schools, not in an urban setting where the norms are a mix of clinical exceptionalism (i.e., the students are seen as too victimized to be held to social norms) and maximal control (i.e., the students are understood as too disruptive to respond to anything but nonreflective adult dominance).

Circle the Wagons: Building Relationships with Teachers

During summer break, before the principal's first year in the school began, a group of teachers visited her home for a summit. The school was in a triage situation, and it was time to circle the wagons. As the ten teachers huddled together for a poolside meeting, the conversations centered on questions about their current mental state and what Green was like. The principal asked them, "How are you all? What's happening at Green?" It was important to respect the teachers' perspectives and experience—and there would be much to learn from them.

Eli, the community coordinator who grew up in the Bronx, told funny stories about the kids and the school security. One student chased a security agent with a fire extinguisher. OK, that story wasn't actually funny, but the way Eli told it made everyone crack up.

After the teachers had all enjoyed a good laugh, Eli brought the group back to reality. "We have one dean in the first-floor hallway and basement and another at the scanning entrance and in the basement, but it's not nearly enough. Our school classrooms are all over the place. No one has time to deal with classroom issues. We spend our time sweeping the hallways, stairwells, and bathrooms, trying to get kids to class. Kids are all over the hallways, all the time."

Ezekiel, a teacher and dean, added, "The staff voted for a third dean and a SAVE [Schools Against Violence in Education] room. This is a common response to behavior issues: hire another person and create another space for kids to be pushed into or pulled out of."

The staff was afraid and needed to be reassured that unacceptable behaviors would not go unpunished. To quickly calm their fears, it was important to reassure this small circle of returning and committed teachers with a clear message that behavior would be everyone's top priority. The principal would be the frontline school culture leader and would guarantee that each unacceptable behavior would not go unpunished. Green's survival depended on the adults getting student behavior under control. Either something terrible would happen to a student, or all the kids and staff would get safety transfers out and then the school would close.

It was especially important to emphasize that student freedom does *not* mean a lack of discipline. Students would be free to the extent that they could balance freedom with self-control around agreed-upon prosocial norms and a social contract.

Freedom and Discipline: You Can't Have One Without the Other

It is worth taking a moment to further unpack the theoretical concepts behind why freedom and discipline, rather than contradict one another, actually complement one another.

- As psychologist Edmund Gordon explained on a visit to the school, "Increasing the disposition to think in pedagogy should be a balance between freedom and control, since real freedom comes from the ability to bring one's own mental abilities under control."
- David Olson's Theory of Self-Control[2] states that self-control is a cognitive problem: or, it's a moral responsibility to oneself. In order to move from agency to self-control, a student must know the rules and be able to express them (this is known as "linguistic compliance"[3]); if there is a breakdown in behavior along the way, it is because there was a breakdown in the rule. It is the teacher's (and principal's) job to help the student and teacher evaluate the "coping mechanisms" that led to the breakdown.
- Paulo Freire talks about the tensions between freedom and discipline: "Authoritarianism and freedom with no boundaries are ruptures in the tense harmony between authority and freedom," and "only in those practices where authority and freedom are preserved in their autonomy (that is the relationship of mutual respect) can we speak of a disciplined practice as well as a practice favorable to the vocation 'to be more.'"[4]
- One thing that sets humans apart from robots is their ability to cooperate, interpret, and achieve shared goals. Homo sapiens are incredibly well adapted to acting and thinking together. Students' ability to act and think in cooperation with others depends on each person's ability to follow a set of agreed-upon rules and norms for collaboration so that everyone benefits from the cooperation.

Michael Tomasello calls this latter theoretical concept, where everyone benefits from the collaboration only if everyone works together (no freeloading allowed!), "mutualism."[5] Therefore, students need to understand that freedom and autonomy are not to be confused with working in isolation or solitude. Even if a student is working independently in the classroom, it's important to realize that people are always interconnected, especially at school.

Students, when they get upset about breaking an agreed-upon school norm, will often say, "I don't care. I only care about myself. I came into this world alone. I will leave this world alone. I don't need anything from anyone." The fact is that people need each other and instinctively want to collaborate. Humans are interdependent, and children learn this at a very young age; and indeed, they will naturally enforce norms of cooperation on others to encourage them to conform to the group as well.[6]

Every child in any public school has the right to learn, and no student has the right to take away someone else's opportunity to learn. And despite their bluster, students want to learn and be part of these social learning groups. Kids really don't want to be on the fringe of the classroom, even though they might say they do.

When given the opportunity and responsibility, students will naturally want to reinforce the rules and norms that enhance cooperation, because this strengthens their group ("we-ness") identities.[7] Students do want to make the cooperative choice and be part of a tight-knit, supportive community.

Thus, establishing a cooperative community with shared goals that learns together means that everyone at the school is responsible for all behaviors. Everyone, not just the counselors, school deans, or assistant principals, must uphold the norms for cooperation and help all students develop self-control inside the classrooms.

Back to the Teachers

This all sounds good in theory, but in action, it was going to be a big shift for the students and teachers at Green. Sitting poolside with the teachers, the principal remembered a conversation she had had recently with the assistant principal at the time about the school's overall discipline culture. The school culture committee had charged him with sharing their plans, which he described by saying, "They worked all summer planning monthly assemblies and whole school field trips across NYC."

This was disturbing to the principal, and it was not the course of action she would have suggested. Learning outside of school was no doubt important, but did people understand how horribly this school had failed children? The changes that needed to be made were not going to be a picnic in the park. There would be no field trips for some time. The staff would first need to figure out how to get the kids into the classrooms, not plan pizza parties, whole-school field trips, and assemblies.

However, it's understandable why the school had taken this approach. Previously, teachers were encouraged to take the kids out for pizza to build relationships and reward students. But, perhaps counterintuitively, this concrete award system would more likely serve to undermine, rather than stimulate, students' altruistic instinct.[8]

To change this current culture around discipline, it was clear that students would need support in learning what to do with freedom and navigating how to act, think, speak, and be responsible in the moment that the discipline infraction occurred inside the classrooms. Students helping other students and becoming positive leaders inside the classrooms would be the key to turning the high school around.

A Fork-in-the-Road Moment

There were many opinions and possibilities for how the new principal might pivot the school. She took a moment to reflect about her next moves, as she sat near the pool under the shade in her backyard with the teachers. She put her four-week-old newborn under her shawl and began to nurse her. The principal's mind continued to wander, as it always did when she nursed. She could hear the commuter train passing on its way up the Hudson River. She tried to get a glimpse of the water through the woods. She had been down this road before at her previous school in Lower Manhattan.

People and organizations, especially large agencies, and in this case, the largest school system in the country, inherently resist change. The status quo is firmly protected. Rather than embrace innovation and encourage principals to take risks in struggling schools and reward them when they do well, the organization or school system labels successful innovators as mavericks who don't assimilate well to the established norms. The reality is any school principal who tries to implement anything perceived by others as unorthodox needs to be fearless, with a will of steel.

The principal wondered, could she get the autonomy she would need from the higher-ups to oversee this turnaround? Did she have the energy to fight the resistance that she knew would be waiting for her at the top? Would she get to see her own three children, all under six years old, at all? Determined to move forward for the children and families in this failed high school, she knew she needed a solid-core crew of teachers and staff who would back her up at every turn.

The Leadership Pivot

She needed to know who, if anyone, was with her, so she said, "Today, you are asking me to hire a third dean. I am not going to hire any more deans. You complained about school security. We won't rely on school security. It's better for everyone that they don't get involved anyway. In fact, I want to go down to one dean."

She looked at Eli and paused. He nodded his head in agreement. No one responded, and the assistant principal kept typing the meeting notes. The principal continued, "The behavior management systems that we use in the school must not be Pavlovic-like systems that minimize the severity of student's needs with their feel-good add-ons like pizza parties, field trips, points systems, tickets, jelly-bean jars, and assemblies. This is patronizing to kids.

Our kids, in general, need way more support than this. All of our systems need to be therapeutic."

She went on: "To start, we need to literally help them make their behaviors conscious. Every single person in the school, including the kids, needs to tackle the maladaptive behaviors, and if we let any behavior slide, like letting a kid barge in and take over your grade meeting, we might as well just advertise in big letters to the whole student body that it is now OK to barge in on staff meetings."

Then, she said, "The kids will fight us really hard when we start to tackle their behaviors, but we cannot back off from doing it or let anything go. We can't ever look past kids wandering the hallways, gambling in the bathrooms, smoking pot in the locker rooms, telling you to suck their dick, standing on tables yelling, ordering burritos from the classroom, throwing food around, not saying something to the student that barges into your meetings, or failing to notice and address behavior in the classroom."

The principal further added, "Also, about pathologizing, rationalizing, or infantilizing kids behaviors . . . we can show sympathy, empathy, and understand the root causes like trauma and poverty, but we can't use them as an excuse to lower the bar and not deal with their behaviors that get in their way, or other people's way, of their rights to learn and their ability to be prosocial and able to cooperate and learn together. That' s a cop-out."

The teachers were still listening attentively, so she continued, "We will be fair and equitable in how we address behaviors. The altruistic prosocial norms, to help, inform, and share,[9] and the Ladder will be our fairness anchor. What I am asking you all to do is going to be really hard for a long time—but then things will improve, I'm sure of it."

At this failed high school, the deans' and counselors' offices would be closed except for mandated counseling and meetings by appointment. Students needed to modify their behaviors with help from their peers. The school would put resources toward providing students with social-emotional support *inside of the classrooms*—and it would be done without hiring more teachers, counselors, or deans. The self-contained, special education, and English language programs that segregate children from their peers would be integrated back into the normal classrooms in socially inclusive groups. The classroom would be *the* place where the therapy and support happens—the classroom itself would be the "SAVE Room."

No one moved or said a word. It seemed that everyone was waiting expectantly for her to continue with her vision, and so she plunged ahead. "We must figure out a way to circle our wagons because this is going to be *work*. If we don't have our arms linked tightly together and have each other's back, we will all be toast." The principal stopped speaking, and there was silence.

Finally, Eli broke through the stunned silence to plan the teacher's first big moves. "So, who are we going to get to back up the teachers in the classrooms then?" The principal was relieved—rather than questioning her approach, Eli was moving ahead to planning the staff's next moves.

Lessons Learned: Empower Teachers to Lead from Day One

Many educators find themselves in situations like this: It's a new principal's first day, no one knows what to think, they've heard the rumors, and many people wonder if should they stay or should they go.

This begs the next question: How does a new principal, joining a failed high school in August, empower the teachers to lead the charge from day one? The extensive interviews done for this book revealed that this meeting was a pivotal moment for all teachers involved. Here, Eli explains that what happened in that meeting at the principal's house empowered him, and so many other teachers, to step up and take responsibility to lead the transformation after that first meeting.

> "The first thing that sticks out to me is that invitation to her house. And she was just like, 'Tell me what is happening. Tell me about the school.' She was just gathering data—she didn't come in with her own agenda. She was open to listening, and I am pretty sure she already knew what she wanted to do in some ways, but she listened to us and our concerns, and we had a dialogue; it was really respectful. The message I got from her that day was, 'I am still the boss, but come talk to me.' It's the same thing as we are asking our students to do: to be open and transparent."

Lessons Learned from the Interviews

- Invite people to a comfortable location outside of school where they can see who the principal is, as a human being. Teachers saw the principal's mother-in-law yell at her for taking her pool umbrella, she nursed her daughter throughout the meeting—and one teacher vacuumed the dirty leaves out of her pool!
- Have a clear vision for what you want to see students doing during each minute of the school day because what students do minute-by-minute during school is what they will get really good at. Keeping this vision front and center will help you listen for the ideas that align with your vision.
- Be able and willing to articulate your vision and belief systems in this first meeting. Be able to support your vision with theory. No one wants to be on a ship without a rudder. People will be happy to see you as a leader with a core guiding principle, on day one, even if they don't necessarily agree with your vision or belief system.

- Being clear-eyed about your vision and belief system gives people the opportunity to leave your school and look for a leader that shares their vision. If that is what feels right to them, it's only fair.
- Make some of the initial big decisions and plan pivotal moves together. This will empower everyone on the staff to lead them.
- Find out who will be your core crew going forward and surround yourself with these people. Don't make a decision without them! One of the principal's teacher leads said jokingly in her interview for this book (and the principal knew she was right), "Whenever the principal made a decision without us, it was a comical disaster!"
- Listen very carefully and figure out how to share common ground and bring others into your vision and belief systems. Again, if people decide they don't fit with the overarching philosophy you are putting into practice, then this frees people to leave and find a leader that shares their vision. That's OK; it's not necessarily personal. Just be transparent about it.
- Spend time listening to people and work hard at drawing their thinking out into the open. So much gets lost in translation from someone else's innermost thoughts to the spoken word to the person on the receiving end of that speech. Making interpretive discourse a norm from the start helps people appreciate how hard it is to communicate effectively.
- Ideas are most successfully built through cooperative problem-solving via interpretive and, often, *uncomfortable* discourse. Try not to dominate any conversation or adhere to strict meeting protocols. Protocols can get in the way of the time and space people need to form ideas and solutions through interpretive discourse. Set aside time for teachers and principals to create new ideas, and solve problems together to be nimble enough to make the tough leadership decisions on a frequent basis throughout the school year.
- Expect people to be ready to back you up with others who may resist the decisions you make, once you decide on your core moves together.
- Don't go into this first meeting, or any meeting, worried about how teachers will rate the school on the anonymous Teacher Survey in February. If a principal is a change agent who is willing to make tough decisions to drive change, you cannot expect everyone to agree with you or even like you. If you are solid and clear in your vision, you feel you are doing the best things for children, and you can support what you are doing with theory, then you should be able to take the heat.
- Be realistic about classroom solutions, and ask, "Can I model this for teachers in classrooms and teach everyone how to do it?" That is, ask yourself, "Can I walk the talk?" If you can't envision yourself doing what you ask teachers to do for two weeks in the classroom and model it with only a moment's notice with a group of ten teachers taking notes and

evaluating you against the teacher evaluation rubrics, then don't ask them to do it.

Before the end of that first meeting, the teachers took the lead in the decision-making process. They decided to program two teachers to be in every classroom. To do this, they agreed to integrate the self-contained 12:1:1 Special Education and English Language programs, which segregate students out of the regular classroom. One teacher boldly backed the principal up by firmly stating, "Self-contained is always a disaster."

So, that was that: They all agreed to amend the student's individual education plans and moved on. The principal continued to be bold in her statements and brave in her assertions: "Teachers hand-holding needs to stop. No more pathologizing or victimizing children. Counselors must not coddle kids. No more hiring more adults to fix kids. Throwing more people at the problem isn't going to work." No one seemed to flinch. They were a team.

Teachers took on official lead roles, and $25,000 was set aside to pay teacher leads overtime pay. A core group of teacher leads in curriculum, behavior, professional development, data management, and strategic planning would be vital to the school's success. Leads would be charged to identify problems, make decisions, run the operations of the school, and be responsible for and held accountable by the staff for implementing all of their agreed-upon (or not) new changes.

Whitney, an algebra teacher and the professional development lead, explains what it was like working with this nontraditional principal: "Every now and then she'd send a frantic email asking if we were keeping track of xyz or if anyone was doing anything, so as a lead, you had to be prepared to show her what was being handled so she didn't have to micromanage you and could do her job."

During that first poolside meeting, these key innovations to help kids thrive were hashed out by the teachers:

- Teacher On Call and The Behavior Conference
- The Circles of Freedom Classrooms
- The Classroom Responsibility Ladder
- The Blue Book Talk: Rules vs. Norms

Later, as the school year progressed, teacher leads would also help develop and implement the following approaches:

- The Principal's Daily Dashboard
- Keepers of the Culture® and Promise Cards
- Dissolving Grades

These later innovations grew out of collaboration and discussion, too. Eventually, these practices in the book would be grouped under the name Learning Cultures®.[10] Learning Cultures® has tangible, workable structures and rubrics that outline the actions and responsibilities for students and teachers in each of the formats.[11]

PART II: BUILDING THE KEY INNOVATIONS TO HELP KIDS THRIVE

Having just listed the key innovations that the teachers discussed at their meeting, this chapter now offers more in-depth overviews of those innovations, with some examples of them in action.

Teacher On Call: Teachers Take Over School Safety

"What if we have all of the teachers *on call* one period a week?" This was the first big pivot point idea that came out of the meeting with the teachers. The on-call teachers would carry a walkie-talkie around, walking the hallways, available to any classroom teacher who needed behavior support. When they were not needed in a specific classroom, on-call teachers would walk the hallways and literally follow kids like "bees on honey" to their classes.

Sometimes it would mean running up and down the many stairwells (A, B, C, or D) and into other schools' hallways on the third, fourth, and fifth floors to herd the kids back into the correct classroom. If called into the classroom, the on-call teacher could take over the teacher's scheduled learning format. This was done for the following reasons:

- to ensure equity of learning; to make sure all student's opportunities to learn were not interrupted by the behavior conference
- to allow *the classroom teacher* to conduct a behavior conference with a disruptive student in the moment
- to give the child an opportunity to mediate their actions around the classroom norms with the teacher and immediately re-engage into the learning format.

The Behavior Conference: Where Students Learn How to Act Responsibly

- In the behavior conference, the classroom teacher sits next to the student, with the behavior conference form and the Blue Book in front of them, and helps the student answer these questions: What happened, described in your own words? What is your side of the story?

- What responsibility (e.g., rule, norm) did this behavior get in the way of? Who broke the rule?
- How did that interfere with your learning or the learning of others?
- What is your responsibility in the future?

The process ends with the student making a verbal commitment and signing the form.

This is a behavior conference Record Sample between a teacher, Jeannie, and the student who threatened her. Teachers conducted about 13,500 classroom behavior conferences per year in the school.

An Example: The Behavior Conference with Jeannie and DeMarco

Every day, in all the teacher's classrooms at Green, teachers engage in intense behavior conferences with students. In the following example, DeMarco sits next to his teacher, Jeannie. This is the beginning of the conference, which is usually the hardest part, when the students are initially resistant to being called out for their behavior.

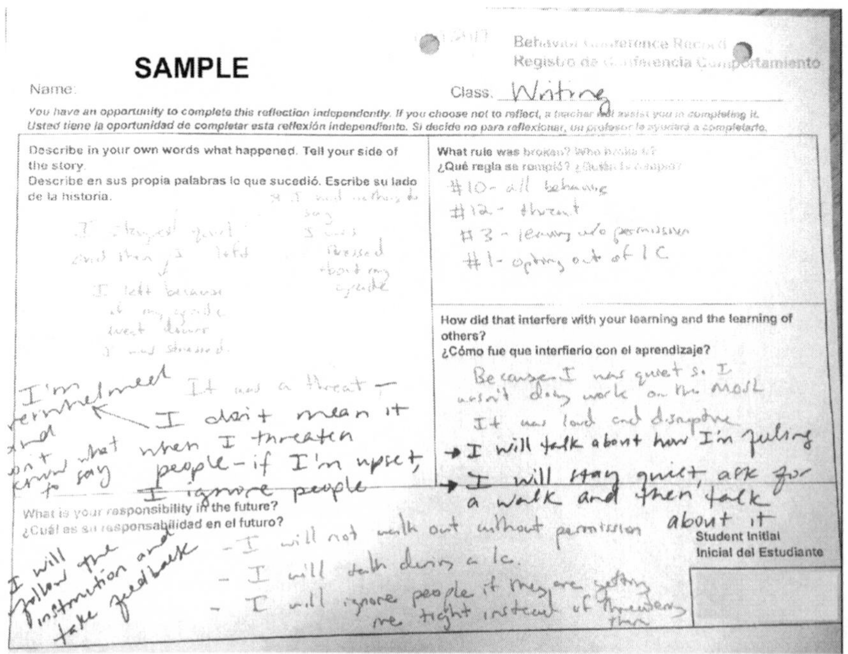

SAMPLE

Registro de Conferencia Comportamiento

Name:

Class: Writing

You have an opportunity to complete this reflection independently. If you choose not to reflect, a teacher will assist you in completing it.
Usted tiene la oportunidad de completar esta reflexión independiente. Si decide no para reflexionar, un profesor le ayudará a completarlo.

Describe in your own words what happened. Tell your side of the story.
Describe en sus propia palabras lo que sucedió. Escribe su lado de la historia.

I'm overwhelmed and don't know what to say

It was a threat — I don't mean it when I threaten people — if I'm upset, I ignore people

What rule was broken?
¿Qué regla se rompió?

#10 - all behaviors
#12 - threat
#3 - leaving w/o permission
#1 - opting out of I C

How did that interfere with your learning and the learning of others?
¿Cómo fue que interfierio con el aprendizaje?

Because I was quiet so I wasn't doing work on the most
It was loud and disruptive
→ I will talk about how I'm feeling
→ I will stay quiet, ask for a walk and then talk about it

What is your responsibility in the future?
¿Cuál es su responsabilidad en el futuro?

I will follow the instruction and take feedback

- I will not walk out without permission
- I will talk during a I C.
- I will ignore people if they are getting me tight instead of threatening them

Student Initial
Inicial del Estudiante

Figure 3.1. Behavior Conference Record

Jeannie: Tell me how we got here [long pause]. What do you remember?

DeMarco: I remember saying, "I don't want to talk to you," because I didn't want to talk to you.

J: Why?

D: I don't remember why I didn't want to talk to you.

J: How were you feeling?

D: How am I feeling now? FULL [It was right after lunch].

J: How *were* you feeling? [Jeannie pulls out the behavior conference record to help DeMarco remember. She started a behavior conference with him that got interrupted, but she was able to capture his earlier statements.] You can use this if you need to. It's your words.

D: I was pissed off.

J: But you were saying you didn't remember.

D: Come on! That was yesterday. Today is a whole new day.

J: Yes, but then you just said to me that I am about to get mad and walk out. That is what you just said to me just now, so there is something you are angry about.

D: I wasn't mad.

J: When we first started, you said this.

D: Oh, well, yeah. Because you 'bout to give me a conference for no reason. I didn't get a move seat at all. [He points to the Behavior Response Ladder, which is on the back of the behavior conference form.]

J: You are right, this is from last time. You are right.

D: But why we going from last time, that is a whole two days ago?

J: The thing is if something happened last class and we didn't resolve it, I have to follow up.

D: You forgive . . .

J: We got up to here last time [points to the Ladder], and we didn't finish because of the bell, and you were like, "Ah, the bell, I have to walk out!"

D: But it doesn't say here [pointing to the Ladder] that if you don't finish a conference, you continue it two days later.

J: So we can't finish this format [the behavior conference] until this is resolved. We need to reflect on these things otherwise. You said, "I am about to get mad," so there is still something that is bothering you.

D: I didn't say I was getting mad. I said I was *about* to get mad.

J: I don't want you to get mad.

D: Right, but I am not mad. I said I was about to get mad.

J: Remember, you were like, you asked me what happened. I showed you how you were arguing with George, and you were like, "That's not my voice!" So, we need to talk about this. Is it alright that I write down you were arguing?

D: Please!

In this exchange, notice how Jeannie, the classroom teacher, doesn't let anything go, and she is the one who spends time helping DeMarco think about his behaviors that got in the way—not a counselor, not the dean or principal. The teacher and the student both get a chance to clarify any confusions or misunderstandings involved in each person's interpretation of the event, in the moment, which allows the teacher and the student to find a way to move forward *together*.

Even though it may seem like lost instruction time, the best way to help a student internalize the norms is for the teacher to sit down and talk with him about his actions and behaviors and come up with a new promise and plan for the future. This approach is grounded in the parenting approach called "inductive parenting,"[12] which assumes that the child wants to be helpful and make the best, most cooperative choices. Parents who communicate with their children about how their behaviors get in the way of getting along with others, and how they can change, are the most effective parents because it encourages the long-term internalization of the societal or group norms.

At Green, so many students displayed classroom behaviors that got in the way of the norms that the teachers needed to massively institute a sort of inductive parenting method to help students learn how to collaborate and socially interact. By creating the teacher on-call system, teachers could sit down and conduct a behavior conference with a student in the moment of the behavior "crisis," all while the student remained within the context of the collaborative peer groups.

Once teachers taught the groups how to cooperate, the human desire to work together provided a gravitational social pull that would absorb almost everyone in the school. With on-call teachers and the behavior conferences in place, teachers averaged two or three of these conferences per day—which amounts to roughly 13,500 per year.

Kate, an English teacher at Green, talks about how she felt when the teachers came up with the idea of an on-call staff at that pivotal meeting discussed earlier in this chapter, and how, in general, the process of teaching was so different from what she ever imagined it would be:

> That was such an exciting moment. I mean, speaking of pivot points. That was real. The people who were around that table. Your willingness to just open your doors and say, "Here I am. I am breastfeeding. I have a newborn baby. Just come on over, and we are going to do this thing." It just felt entirely overwhelming. But, that first conversation is where On Call came from. And there were other things. Just ideas that came from that meeting. On Call was huge. Eli and Ezekiel said that we need help, and they had the idea, they stated the need. You remember what it was like; kids were running the hallways. It was chaos, absolute chaos. Everybody was like, "We don't know what to do." On Call has such a dual purpose; you clear the hallways, and then you are available to come in and be a behavior support in the classroom.

The Circles of Freedom Classrooms: No More Kicking Kids Out of Classrooms

At the summer meeting, Kate had explained that, "There was always a party going on in the hallways. At least half of the kids roamed the halls, and many of those students never went to class." The classrooms, not the hallways, needed to be the places where students roamed free. Kate explains the thinking behind the second and third big moves that came out of the meeting: the Circle of Freedom Classrooms and the Classroom Responsibility Ladder.

> So many of the teachers were kicking kids out of class or happily letting them leave. Within the classroom, there were such dramatic behavior challenges, and we didn't have a way to handle them. Even myself, as a teacher who wants to support and teach and believes every child can learn and should be in an integrated classroom, I wanted a place to send them. I wanted to be able to kick them out of my room! That was the frustration. I was like, "I don't know what to do with them. I don't have a tool. I don't have anything in my classroom. So why can't I call? Where is my rubber room?" We didn't know that there was another way. That was the big pivot point for me as a teacher, and I think for a lot of us—shifting that perspective to reintegrate them into learning exists inside the classroom. Sending them out is not going to solve any problems. And we didn't send them out because we didn't have anywhere to send

> them to except into the chaos of the hallway, which they would help themselves to freely. They were very happy out there.

If classrooms could be "Circles of Freedom," where actions are within students' own control rather than dictated by teachers, then maybe that would encourage kids to stay inside them. The teachers decided that if all the classrooms could be Circles of Freedom, that might encourage kids to stay inside them. In the school's Circles of Freedom classrooms, students would be able to do the following:

- move around the room and talk to one other;
- breach and determine their own teaching points;
- talk at the precise moment that they recognized their own confusion or needed to say something;
- reach out into their environment and ask for help;
- control the information they encountered and processed because they would be able to choose their own texts;
- use their language to think in cooperative groups; and
- flow in and out of self-chosen groups to learn cooperatively, because working cooperatively is where most of the higher-order thinking happens.

Because the person who determines what is relevant to read, write, and learn ultimately holds the power, in the Circle of Freedom classrooms, students determine their own reference points and goals for learning.[13] Much like when a toddler first begins to point at objects in their environment and seeks out a caregiving adult to jointly attend, student intentions initiate action in the classrooms. Students become agents of their learning by initiating all actions and choosing the point of reference.

The School-Wide Blue Book Talk: Rules vs. Norms

"Are these good rules to live by?" The third big move decided on during the meeting was to create the school norms. The practice of freedom would require students to take on many responsibilities, and the students would need to agree to a set of school responsibilities as "good rules to live by."

To do this, it would be important for the leadership and the students to spend the first two weeks together engaged in a "Blue Book Talk." The teachers and staff would surround the principal while she did these talks in each classroom, in a show of support, ensuring that the message would get across to every single child.

The Blue Book talk would do two things:

1. Describe the classrooms as Circles of Freedom where students exercise their right to learn and have freedom of mind, voice, and movement; and
2. Explain that every single student would need to agree to the student responsibilities as "good rules to live by" so that the rules could eventually become the agreed-upon norms, upheld by all.

As David Olson suggests in his work, the teachers decided that the school norms would not be regulative rules, such as traffic rules; rather, they would merely highlight the students' responsibilities to each other. The leadership, teachers, and other students would actively hold all students accountable under their rights and responsibilities as detailed in the Blue Book.

Conveniently, the responsibilities were grounded in the altruistic prosocial norms to help, inform, and share,[14] introduced earlier in this chapter and provided again here for reference. Some of those responsibilities include:

- attend school regularly, and make every effort to achieve;
- respect the dignity and equality of others and refrain from conduct that denies or impinges on the rights of others;
- be polite, courteous, and respectful toward others regardless of actual or perceived age, race, creed, color, gender, gender identity, gender expression, religion, national origin, citizenship/immigration status, weight, sexual orientation, physical and/or emotional condition, disability, marital status, and political beliefs, and refrain from making slurs based on these criteria;
- behave in a polite, truthful, and cooperative manner toward students and school staff;
- promote good human relations and build bridges of understanding among the members of the school community;
- use non confrontational methods to resolve conflicts; and
- provide leadership to encourage fellow students to follow established school policies and practices.

Page 18 of the Blue Book.

It was important to explain to the students the concept of educational privilege versus educational rights and to help them know about their educational worth. Taxpayers pay over $100 a day for student's right to learn, or $250,000 per kid by high school graduation. The dean at Green agreed with this path and suggested, "Let's show the kids a picture of a Lamborghini car at this point so that they know how much they're worth." Once presented with this information, a student who was struggling to graduate, shouted, "Oh man, I'm just a school bus!"

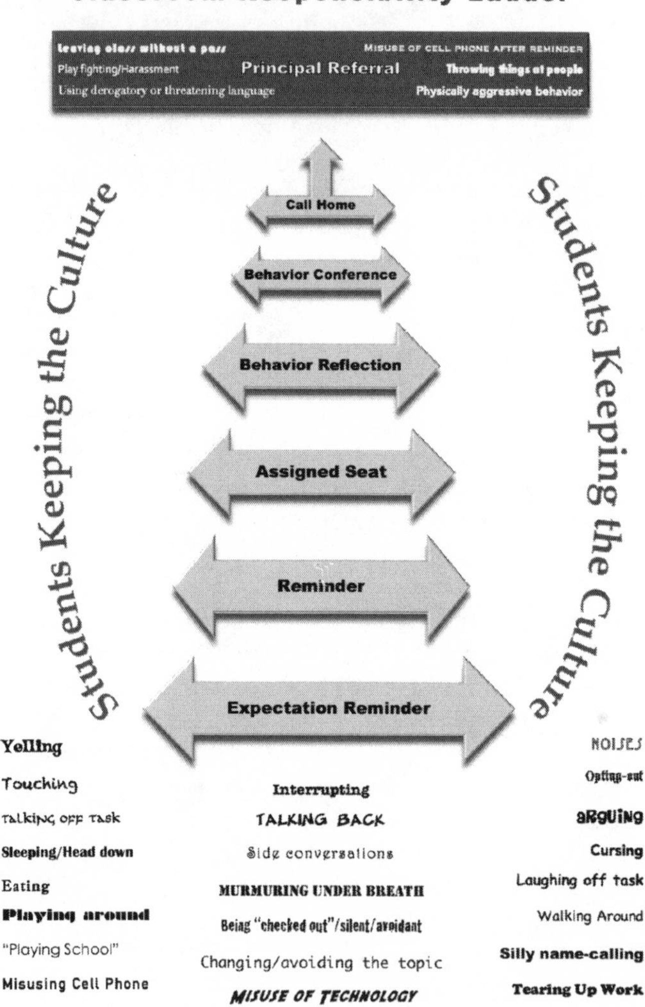

Figure 3.2. The Classroom Responsibility Ladder

The Classroom Responsibility Ladder: A Student's Due Process Rights

Once the students agreed that the Blue Book-designated responsibilities would be good norms to uphold, the principal, the students, and the teachers needed to create the agreed-upon school-wide Classroom Responsibility Ladder (see figure 3.2). The Classroom Responsibility Ladder is how students would learn to take responsibility for their own practice of freedom inside the classroom. Following the steps up to the top of the Ladder would not be about giving out punishments; rather, it would be about helping the students and teachers change their own behavior in the moment; to learn self-control and self-regulation in the moment of a behavior crisis.

The Classroom Responsibility Ladder provided:

- guideposts, because it included concrete steps that the teachers and students followed to teach students how to practice freedom responsibly;
- due process, because it gave students space to make mistakes in the process of learning how to be free and responsible, before punishing them for infringements; and
- a safe harbor, because it enhanced the sense of a "we-ness"[15] culture in the school.

Creating this Ladder with the students is when the fun begins. The principal starts out by asking the students, "What are all the behaviors that kids do in the classrooms at Green that get in the way of your Blue Book responsibilities?" It helps to offer possible examples, to help the kids feel comfortable offering their own answers: "Do you throw food? Do you say 'shut up' to each other? Do you wander around the classroom? Do you put your head down on the desk and sleep? Do you zone out and think about pizza? Do you only pretend to listen? Do you say things under your breath when you get angry? Do you fiddle with the paper on your desk instead of reading the words on the page?"

Kids start to have fun admitting all their poor behaviors, and it's a good idea to let them enjoy this process. It is important to bring out all of the behaviors that get in the way of them carrying out their responsibilities, so that everyone can all agree on which of their actions do the most harm. The students often have disputes around this.

For example, without fail, when some students bring up "laughing" as a disruptive behavior, others inevitably argue about why laughing is a problem: "We like to laugh, and we laugh out loud; what is wrong with that?" There are many ways to intend a laugh and to interpret a laugh (e.g., sarcasm, avoidance, bullying, happiness, embarrassment, etc.), so it's worth a discussion. After all, a child could be thinking, "Did she laugh at me or with me?" or "Is she making fun of me?" A teacher could think, "Are they laughing to avoid the work or start something with someone?"

Once the kids finish their list of negative behaviors, ask them, "Since learning is your responsibility, and you will learn to back each other up and work as a community in here, what can you all do to help remind other students to stop doing these things that get in the way?"

At first, kids won't like this idea of backing each other up at all. They see it as snitching. Kids will vehemently disagree with this suggestion and say things like, "My behavior is my business. I mind my own business and no one else's," "People have to help themselves," "I don' t snitch," "I come into this world by myself; I take care of myself, that is all," "If they are in trouble, that is their issue, not mine. Why would I make it my issue?," and "That makes no sense at all."

It's important to prepare an agreed-upon staff rebuttal to this inevitable argument:

"Wouldn't you want to be helped out by a student before a teacher takes you up the Ladder? Reminding each other helps you from getting into more trouble. It saves students from the teacher needing to get up and come over to their seat. And if you help someone one day, they might help you the next day. It's about protecting each other. It's about helping each other stay in the Circles of Freedom. It's your due process rights as a student and protects you from student and teacher tyranny. You know how segregation begins? By getting kicked out of class. Don't let each other get kicked out of class. Each of you all belong here every single minute."

Teachers initially often do not like to address behavior this way. Some say it gives students way too many chances. Others use it as a punishment and cannot see it as a way to teach students how to conform their behaviors with the agreed-upon norms. Some think the whole idea of the norms as responsibilities and consequences for noncooperators, or that the idea of white teachers calling students of color out on behavioral norms is racist, because it perpetuates the white supremacist norms that keep people oppressed.

It's important to make the distinction between the norms of a white supremacist culture that perpetuates a system of oppression and the agreed-upon rules that become prosocial norms for cooperation, which are grounded in the altruistic human norms of helping, informing, and sharing. Agreeing upon rules that become norms to live by is different than saying to kids, "You have to act white."

Getting teachers to value the fact that students need time and a ton of support to learn how to practice freedom and act responsibly is one of the hardest things to teach teachers how to do in the classrooms comfortably and enthusiastically. In fact, for this reason and a few more, the system was purposely designed to not solely rely on teachers to implement behavior turnarounds. For one thing, it's much more natural for the kids to want to create a we-ness[16] identity with each other inside the classrooms. It's more promising to rely heavily on a child's natural cooperative instinct to monitor the norms and hold their peers accountable for following them.

Also, let's be clear, it was about pure numbers: simply put, there were more students who could notice and address behaviors than teachers. The students were not only better at noticing the behaviors, but also, the other kids responded to student reminders better than they did to teachers' reminders. Once teachers taught the students how to reinforce the norms, the students took over the classroom behavior management. Here is how it might go with a teacher noticing and addressing behavior:

"Jake, you're talking about eating pizza at lunch with Benedict. What rule is your behavior breaking? Let's read the rules together. That's right, rule #2. You are supposed to be talking with your group about the breach. What can you do to change your behavior around rule #2? This is your second reminder. Right? Let's look at the Ladder together; your first reminder came from Ezekiel when he asked you to read in sync with the group. The next time it will be a move seat, and you will need to switch your chair around and sit at a different spot at your Unison Reading table."

Once students realize the fairness and due process of the Ladder system, they develop a love-hate relationship with it. The kids will want the teacher to follow the Ladder fairly and equitably, but at the same time, they will probably also argue when the teacher goes too quickly up it! But, at least, the student is showing an interest and investment in the Ladder as a fair contract.[17]

The Principal's Daily Dashboard Hour

Once the principal, students, and staff agreed on the rules, those rules became the school norms. When teachers began to use the Classroom Responsibility Ladder, students who did not respond after six chances would be referred to the principal. In the beginning, since every behavior would be noticed and addressed, the principal referrals were coming in fast and furious. The principal needed to build a system of administrative response, or the whole classroom behavior system would fail.

The administrative response protocol to behavior was:

- Once a student got to the top of the Ladder, after experiencing six chances to change, the teacher would send a referral to the principal.
- This comment would be forwarded directly to the principal's dashboard.
- In order to respond immediately, the referral would need to be written so that the principal could visualize exactly what happened in the classroom.
- At the beginning of the school year, once referrals started to show up, the principal and deans would walk around the hallways with their computer in hand, open to the dashboard comments.
- Once a principal referral came onto the principal's dashboard, the administrative team would find the student in the hallway or wait for them to exit the class and read the comment with them.

This process, of the principal responding directly to behaviors in the moment, was a pivotal first move that sent shock waves through the school community. Students quickly realized that there would be swift and forceful administrative responses to the classroom behaviors.

This is how the Daily Behavior Dashboard would play out:

- The teacher would write the principal an on-the-spot anecdote from their classroom if a student did not self-regulate after six reminders (a verbal reminder, a directive to move their seat, on-call teacher intervention, behavior reflection, behavior conference, and a call home).
- The principal would get an email and sometimes, if she could, wait for the student at the end of class.
- Every day at 9:00 am and 2:00 pm, the behavior team (principal, deans, and assistant principals) would meet to review the day's principal referrals and resolve each one.

Here are a few examples of some of the typical teacher referrals that the principal and deans would read daily: "Student A went up the Ladder for not being cooperative during Unison, refusing responsibilities for Unison. When given reminders by his group member, he would ignore it or respond with un-promotive tones, gestures, and comments (mumbling, looking away, sarcasm). He also had reminders from the mini-lesson, and when his un-promotive behavior continued, he got up to a move seat on the Ladder, which he refused. He filled out the reflection, but again did not resume Unison with his group, getting to a behavior conference.

"He was uncooperative during this, though he made it to the end with the goal of following Unison norms. He got up to 'call home' on the Ladder when he was cursing while other students were getting reminders, saying, 'This bitch just can't stand being wrong,' and 'What the fuck,' mumbling curses afterward (principal referral). I will call home about his behavior in class."

Here is another sample: "Student B got up to principal referral for being on social media (like Facebook), texting, going on games, accessing videos not related to content, talking off task, ignoring reminders, and talking back when given reminders ('Leave me alone, boy' or 'Don't look at me'). He escalated his behavior to being dismissive and telling me to go away, to not look at him, to 'Pay attention to your fucking kids,' and then they started calling out 'Suck my dick' to other students and muttering more curses under his breath. He was throwing stickies with his table and was off task the whole two hours. He was getting up and bothering students to try and get attention."

As is evident from these examples, the teachers took the process of responding to behaviors according to the Behavior Response Ladder very seriously—and because of this, the kids did too.

PART III: THE PRINCIPAL ESTABLISHED HERSELF AS A FRONTLINE SCHOOL CULTURE LEADER

The students started to swiftly realize that the principal did not let any behaviors go. When this happened, students quickly became more self-aware of how their own behaviors were infringing upon their own responsibilities (i.e., norms), and the school pivoted.

Trevor and his Encounter with the Daily Dashboard Tracker

Trevor ran himself up the Classroom Responsibility Ladder in all of his classes, so it was necessary for someone to confront him and let him know this right away. For example, at the start of the school year, Naina Vohra, an Environmental Science teacher, sent the principal a referral during class through the dashboard. The principal received it before the end of the period, ran down to the classroom, and waited outside the door for Trevor. As Trevor exited, the principal called out his name. Once the hallways cleared out, Trevor went over to the principal.

"What happened in Vohra's class just now?" she asked.

"Nothing. What are you talking about?"

"I have her write-up right here on my dashboard." This was an entirely new concept for the students, and Trevor's jaw dropped. "What? What comment? When? How did she write that? I just came out of her classroom!"

"I know. She wrote it in class once you got to the Principal Referral part of the Ladder. You know, you had six chances to change your behavior, and you didn't, so she wrote a referral."

"I didn't see her do that! What did she say? Let me see it!"

"I will read it with you. Come take a look." They went to the principal's office together.

After they read the comment, he got defensive and mad at the teacher. This process might encourage students to retaliate against teachers, but it's important that the students have access to their information, especially anything about their own behaviors, in a principal referral. With the information, the student has more power over his or her actions. This access also sends the message that everyone in the school is interconnected, and the agreed-upon norms need to be upheld by all. This commitment requires the principal to follow up on every referral. Otherwise, the Ladder would be just a ladder to nowhere.

She asked Trevor, "What about this comment is false?"

"I didn't tell the teacher to 'Shut the fuck up.'" Now he was getting defensive. This was good. He didn't like how his own words sounded when he read them out loud together with the principal.

"Should we ask the teacher?"

"No, I don't want to talk to her. She's lying. She is a liar."

"You think so? Why would she make this up? Here's what we can do. Let's go talk to her. If you two can agree on what you actually said, then I will resolve this comment, and we can both move on with our lives today, OK?"

The teacher was a little surprised to see the principal talking with Trevor so soon after she wrote up the comment. The principal started out by saying, "Naina, Trevor and I saw your comment. He's pretty upset about it. Trevor, tell her."

"Nah, no, no, I am not talking to her. I didn't say anything."

Naina replied, "You said it, Trevor. Do you want me to get other students to back that up?"

"No."

The principal didn't want this to be a long back-and-forth, so she took this as Trevor's admission of guilt and said, "The point of all this today, Trevor, is that your words matter. What you say matters. If you say something like, 'Shut the fuck up,' it gets in the way." And since she always had her Blue Book with her, she opened it to page 18 (see figure 2.3) so that Trevor, Naina, and the principal could read over the responsibilities out loud together and find the ones that his behavior undermined.

"Trevor, let 's read, all together, the student responsibilities section of the Blue Book again on page 18. Remember this? Stop when you find the responsibilities your behavior got in the way of today in class."

All three read together in sync, and he stopped at responsibility #10: "Behave in a manner that is polite, truthful, and cooperative towards students and school staff."

The principal said, "OK, good. Can you do that next time?"

Trevor said, "Maybe, depends on if Vohra gets me tight again."

"Telling her to 'shut the fuck up' gets in the way of your responsibilities, and you promised to uphold these, that they were important for us to follow at this school. Didn't you agree to these, Trevor? Remember my Blue Book Talks?"

"Yeah."

She let it go at that, but she knew the road would be long with Trevor. Although his referrals didn't end, he at least stopped getting a principal referral in every class.

Here is what another student, Naya, said when asked about the principals' habit of walking around the school with her computer and Blue Book:

> **Naya**: Every time I got in trouble, you brung out that Blue Book! I already know about the Blue Book because I saw it in middle school, but not to the extent where it was, like, every time it was a problem, I had to read something from the Blue Book. I was not aware of my student

responsibilities, and I was never aware of what my role is as a student in this school so every time there was a situation or there was a mediation or I knew some information, the Blue Book was brought out, and I was always like, "Wow, I was never aware of that." I was never aware of what can happen. Or how, if I get into a fight, these are a list of consequences that are supposed to happen. I was never really aware of the Blue Book, so when I came here, I was, like, every situation was, like, 'Let's look at the Blue Book,' 'Oh, let's look at the Blue Book.' So, it was just, like, now I can really identify that, OK, I do have a responsibility to report any fight that is supposed to happen. I do have a responsibility as a student in a high school.

Principal: What would I really focus on? I didn't focus on the consequences with you guys; what did I focus on?

N: Mostly the actions. Not really the consequences, but the student responsibilities always.

Principal: Remember how you used to make fun of me because I always had the Blue Book with me?

N: Yes, and that laptop.

Depending on the behavior and the amount of recidivism of the behavior, the principal employed many different ways to address the principal referrals. Here are a few:

- Read the referral out loud so the student can hear how their behavior sounds to others outside of the classroom, and help them make a promise to change, putting it in writing.
- Bring the student or group of students up to the principal's office to read the Blue Book, specifically page 18, and identify all the responsibilities their behaviors impede.
- Call the family together from the principal's office and discuss the behaviors, find the responsibility the behavior impeded, come up with a promise to change, a plan, and ways everyone can help students achieve their promise to change.
- Suspend or remove the student, depending on the infraction.
- Ask the student what she thinks should happen as a consequence.

Teachers had their own reactions to these new policies and processes:

Whitney: For me, knowing the way the principal had our back, that was huge. I knew what it meant to follow the Ladder, and I knew I could trust the principal to do her part. We all had responsibilities, and the clarity made it so much safer.

Eli: The first two weeks of school, how can we forget about the principal's social norms talks? The principal created this situation where she went into every single classroom and co-created the Ladder with the students. Talk about Principaling 101—the principal is having this conversation with the kids about it? They get to butt heads with the principal right then and there. "You don't like it? Let's talk it out," which is what we tell them, and we are going to come to a place of agreement. Then we will move forward and work together for the rest of the school year. That needs to happen in every school. The principal needs to go into every classroom. 'You have seen me suspend someone. I am the principal, and here is my mindset [Classrooms as Circles of Freedom], how do you want to protect this mindset?' That is where the restorative Response Ladder came from. Visiting this every year and having this become a living document is very important for the student population because they then can control their own behavior and how the teachers are expected to hold them accountable.

Kate: It is so interesting to look back now that we have mostly fixed the problem. It's hard to even access how unsolvable and impossible the problem felt now that there is order. Your house was so welcoming. It's something I think about a lot actually and is the sort of do-it-yourself, "we are figuring this out" on our own quality of starting a new, small school. This is something that it took me some time to get used to.

Kate: When I became a teacher, I thought someone would give me an instruction manual, right? And that's just not the case. Particularly, there is not an instruction manual for teaching, certainly not one that works. And there is not an instruction manual for the single right way to run a school, and it took me a while to get comfortable with that. And now it's part of what I love most about this work; that we are always tinkering because there is nothing written in stone; it's never boring. You are always creating and improving and figuring a different and better way and refining things. It took me some time to get used to. I am not quite as, "Let's just dive in headfirst" like our principal was, but I needed her energy.

Although implementing a pedagogy of freedom is a big learning curve for both teachers and students, the payoff is worth it.

NOTES

1. Cynthia McCallister, 2018, https://cynthiamccallister.com/.
2. David R. Olson, "A New Theory of Agency and Responsibility," Learning Cultures, 2014, https://www.youtube.com/watch?v=x5wwt7l8Lmc.
3. Scientific experiments have shown that people who make a verbal commitment are 50 percent more likely to resist the temptation to break their promise (e.g., promising not to eat the candy on the table until after dinner). Olson, "A New Theory of Agency and Responsibility."
4. Paulo Freire, *Pedagogy of Freedom: Ethics, Democracy, and Civic Courage* (Lanham, MD: Rowman & Littlefield Publishers, 1998), 83.
5. Michael Tomasello, *Why We Cooperate* (Boston: MIT Press, 2009), 54.
6. Michael Tomasello, *Becoming Human: A Theory of Ontogeny* (Cambridge, MA and London, England: Harvard University Press, 2019), 256–57.
7. Tomasello, *Why We Cooperate*, 47–50.
8. Ibid., 23.
9. Tomasello studied what enables humans to cooperate; he learned that humans are altruistic-helping-informing-sharing, and because of this altruism, early humans exploited this capacity and placed special preference on how their actions and the actions of others can benefit the group (i.e., cooperation), with their main goal being survival.
10. McCallister, 2018, https://cynthiamccallister.com/.
11. Theory: Jerome Bruner defines "formats" as embedded support systems "in routinized, highly recurrent settings" (i.e., "childhood mealtime, dressing, and bedtime rituals"; "book reading" routines; "greeting/farewell"; and "polite request"). Formats "provide familiar settings for mother and child" (teacher and student) to know "what they have 'on their minds' and, above all, what is to be accomplished." Acting in a format "hands the child a comprehensible context on a silver platter, and concretely provides him or her with the support for making meaning" (Janet W. Astington, David R. Olson, and Philip David Zelazo, *Developing Theories of Intention: Social Understanding and Self-Control* [New York, Psychology Press, 2009], 336).
12. "Much research has shown that so-called inductive parenting—in which adults communicate with children about the effects of their actions on others and about the rationality of cooperative social action—is the most effective parenting style to encourage internalization of societal norms and values." From Tomasello, *Why We Cooperate*, 50–51.
13. "Acting intentionally is what grants autonomy and freedom to the doer; one is free to the extent that one's own actions are intentional, in one's own control, rather than caused, forced, or prescribed by another . . . it is this autonomy that allows the formation of unique personal identity, a self." From David R. Olson, *Psychological Theory and Educational Reform: How School Remakes Mind and Society* (Cambridge, UK: Cambridge University Press, 2003), 145.
14. Tomasello studied what enables humans to cooperate; he learned that "humans are altruistic-helping-informing-sharing," and because of this altruism, early humans exploited this capacity and placed special preference on how their actions and the actions of others can benefit the group (i.e., cooperation), with their main goal being survival.
15. Tomasello, *Why We Cooperate* and Tomasello, *Becoming Human*.
16. Ibid.
17. The inception story of the Classroom Responsibility Ladder can be found at Cynthia McCallister, *Unison Reading: Social Inclusive Group Instruction for Equity and Achievement* (New York: Corwin Press, 2011), 96–103.

Chapter Four

Think

Educational policymakers and institutional leaders often pay lip service to the idea of freedom as essential to a good education. However, in practice, freedom-based approaches are often resisted by those in charge. Freedom-based practices require a significant change in attitude and focus on the part of teachers, administrators—and also the students themselves. Indeed, the most resistance can sometimes come from students, such as Jayden in this chapter, who found it easier to complete worksheets and teacher-directed assignments rather than engage in a conscious decision-making process around what to learn and read. This is not surprising, given that American schools are generally organized around memorization, leveled reading, and other teacher-directed, rote learning practices. However, these practices do little to teach students how to think, which should be the focus of the educational system.

Perhaps nowhere is the lack of freedom more apparent than in the practice of leveled reading. At Green, nearly all of the students were reading at very underperforming levels. The new principal's answer was a multipronged, perhaps counterintuitive, overhaul of the reading program: Students began to choose their own texts to read, to read them together in their own groups, and to discuss their own questions and opinions about the texts in detail. After this approach was implemented, students at Green saw a marked improvement in their reading grades and their test scores.

Like students, teachers can also be resistant to freedom-based approaches and practices. At Green, teachers had to adapt to a very different teaching environment under the new principal. Teacher-mandated texts and essay prompts were eliminated, as were worksheets and PowerPoint presentations. Teachers no longer chose texts for students—not even texts that teachers offered because they thought they spoke to students' cultural identities (such as assigning an article on the Black Lives Matter movement to an African American student). Even such well-meaning actions undermine students' ability to make independent choices based on their own preferences. Allowing students to choose their own texts to read in schools is fundamental to them forming their own unique identities in a student-driven school. Even though it's hard for teachers to give up the power to direct learning and choose class texts, the teachers at Green came to appreciate this opportunity to shift their own perspectives about their roles in the classroom, and what it truly means to be an effective teacher.

"The oppressed, having internalized the image of the oppressor and adopted his guidelines, are fearful of freedom. Freedom would require them to eject this image and replace it with autonomy and responsibility. Freedom is acquired by conquest, not by gift. It must be pursued constantly and responsibly. Freedom is not an ideal located outside of man; nor is it an idea which becomes myth. It is rather the indispensable condition for the quest for human completion."[1] —Paulo Freire

Freedom is at the core of everyone's approach at Green. Although this sounds straightforward, in reality, freedom-based practices are often questioned in school settings. Freedom is preached and valued at the highest levels of the leadership system, but once people see it in action, it is often resisted by administrators, teachers, staff members—and students.

Several of the fundamental tenets of a freedom-based approach were illustrated in action in chapter 2, in the case of Esteban. This chapter begins with the voices of several students and the on-the-ground impact of these policies on the people who matter the most in any school: the kids. Then, the concrete actions employed by teachers and the principal at Green to create and encourage this atmosphere of freedom—actions always undergirded by the Five Principles of Freedom (Think, Build, Act, Speak, and Fight)—are discussed.

The principal sat down with a group of seniors—Naya, Sallie Mae, and Johancarla—who had all been freshmen when the principal started at Green, to find out how the shift toward a pedagogy of freedom looked and felt to them. She began the group conversation by saying, "I want to go deep. Let's talk about freedom."

> **Naya**: Before I came here, I never heard of doing school this way. It was a brand-new way of teaching, like a whole new system, with new rules, new principles. Coming here and just knowing that my education is not as controlled—I have control, and I have a say in how I am being taught and what I am going to learn. Everything was different.
>
> I was so used to having a traditional setting with a teacher who told me what to do, and I had worksheets and word problems. But here, it was just different. I have control over what I am learning. If I know it takes this amount of time to learn this topic, then I will take this amount of time to learn it. Also, I can get help and information from my peers versus me always having to ask the teacher.

Sallie Mae: Or I go to the Internet. I can use my resources. We got books that help us in Math and US History; we got a lot of resources.

Naya: We have standards. We make our own questions. Like, if I am reading a standard, for example, and I don't understand what World War II is about or what happened, I can make my own questions from that. Like, what happened in World War II, how did it happen, what led to it, how did it affect people? Like, I can make my own list of questions and not have to rely on the teacher to give me a list of questions, and then I have to answer her list of questions. It's about me making a list of questions myself about what I want to understand about that standard.

Johancarla: At first, I was confused, and I didn't think this would benefit me in any way. But, eventually, I learned that I could learn from other people as well as *bounce ideas off of other people.* Overall, this has helped me, especially outside of school, because before, I could not communicate effectively with other people.

So, although in retrospect Naya, Sallie Mae, Johancarla, and many other students at Green came to value their freedom, initially, many students actively resisted and resented this opportunity to be free in school.

JAYDEN REFUSES FREEDOM OF MIND

Jayden, a tenth-grade student, could be heard crying in the counselor's office. His voice echoed down the hallway as he exclaimed, "I just want to do my work!" Upon further questioning, he elaborated on the cause of his distress: "The middle school I came from, they would give us a piece of paper, and you got to do that for class. And then they give you another piece of paper, and they'd be like, 'Hey, this is homework.' So, when I first came here, I was like, 'I gotta teach myself?' I was like, 'I don't know, I don't think this is how it goes.' Like, the lesson—they don't tell us like what we are doing today. They don't teach us on the topic. At my middle school, they would be like, 'We are doing this today, and this is what you are going to learn.' I am used to that, why can't I do that? Why is this school so different? At all the other schools in the city, they do a lesson, they give you a worksheet, I do my work, I get a grade on it, and I am done. I do good in schools like that!"

Jayden was referring to an all-too-ubiquitous approach to education: the banking concept of learning that seeks to control how and what students think. The principal waited to make sure Jayden was finished, and then she said, "I know. So, you are telling me you like to be told what to do?"

He nodded and said, "Yes."

"You mean that you like learning only about the topic on the worksheet the teacher gives you?"

"YES!"

"You mean that you like to answer the teacher's questions?"

"YES!"

"You mean you don't want to ask your own questions, choose your own texts to read, and talk to others to figure out what things mean?"

He looked down and said, "I just want to do my work. I just want to sit in the lesson, find out what I need to know, finish the worksheets, and be out. I just want to DO . . . MY . . . WORK!"

The principal said to Jayden, with a look of concern on her face, "Your last school *did not* teach you how to think. Filling out worksheets or packets is not going to get you to think for yourself. You won't free your mind this way. Worksheets are like chains; they keep your mind locked up. Don't you want to be free to think for yourself? Do you always want to be dependent on someone else's version of what you should know and how you should learn? Don't you want to ask your own questions, search for and read your own texts? That school didn't teach you how to think. That's a problem."

Students truly did not know how to take responsibility for their own learning. They couldn't ask themselves, *How do I know what I don't know? How do I ask a good question? How can I find the answers to my own questions? How do I know when I know something?*

And really, given the state of the educational system, why would students know how to ask those questions and answer them for themselves? Classroom practices that undermine a student's agency are one huge obstacle, but this vignette illustrates another undercurrent that the students had to swim against: well-meaning adults who lower the expectations (or patronize kids) when students show signs of struggle or resistance.

FREEDOM: THE KEY TO A TWENTY-FIRST-CENTURY EDUCATION

One might think that students would want to be free to think for themselves, but they often resist it fiercely, as the exchange with Jayden illustrates. It is hard for children to break free from oppressive school practices, though it is important for the future of our country that they do so.

People expect US schools to teach children how to think—but children thinking for themselves in school, creatively and independently, is not the norm. David R. Olson explains one of the many reasons why our schools get in the way of a children's freedom of mind: "E. D. Hirsch (1987), whose listing of what every child needs to learn has become a model for the Core Curriculum, completely overlooks the concepts critical to metacognitive thought such as assume, conclude and hypothesize. It appears to sponsor a school for traditional knowledge acquisition rather than a school for thinking."[2]

At Green, teachers actively transitioned the students away from memorization and rote learning practices and toward learning how to think. One of the physics teachers, Chris Bohl, explains how this process looked in his classroom: "Making higher-level research questions is not a problem anymore. That used to be a huge problem. Teaching them the why and how, and synthesizing questions rather than just asking, 'What is an aqueduct?' That was a huge part. There were many lessons about what makes an interesting or higher-level question. What is the difference between trivia and an actually useful fact or useful information about a process that they can apply to other things? So, like generalizing your knowledge in some way. So, you found out how an aqueduct worked, but how does that explain how other processes work that you are familiar with now?

"What we do a lot of is just teaching people how to think. Whether or not they come away with an understanding of how potential energy becomes kinetic energy is not, it is nice if they know it, but the goal of the course is to figure out how to plan something, figure out how to ask good questions about it, figure out how to research it, and figure out how you know if you have learned something new and how to apply it to new situations."

Schools continue to feed children information from the teacher and a limited range of approved texts as if it were still 1890. But 1890 was, of course, before the Internet, TV, the telephone, YouTube, and Google. Then, teachers, professors, politicians, and religious leaders functioned as gatekeepers controlling the flow of knowledge and information. But with free access to knowledge in the twenty-first century, upholding the standard of the teacher as an all-knowing gatekeeper who disseminates information is simply no longer the best approach to education.

CHOOSING TO READ: LITERACY IN A TEXTUAL/INTERPRETIVE COMMUNITY

Imagine a mother home with her eighteen-month-old toddler. The child brings her mother five self-chosen books: *Room on the Broom*, *Spinky Sulks*, *I Went Walking*, *Elmo's ABC Book*, and *Happy Birthday to You!*. Most of these books are way beyond her prescribed reading level. That sentence sounds silly in this context, doesn't it?

What's wrong with reading *Room on the Broom* or *If You Give A Mouse A Cookie* to a toddler who can barely speak, let alone read? Surely the child is absorbing the sounds, the images, and the details. And what better way to cultivate a love of reading than to allow children to choose their own reading material?

If a mother wouldn't turn an eighteen-month-old child away from a challenging, or any, book at home, then why would a teacher do this to a school-age child? Across the country, schools sort students in classrooms according to each student's prescribed or "formulaic" reading level, starting in kindergarten.

Once neatly sorted into leveled groups, teachers don't let students choose their own texts to read outside of their independent or "just right" reading level. It's no wonder US schools rank just above average. Schools steal children's autonomy away and force them out of being able to read interesting or challenging books at age five, just when they start to flourish and develop their Theory of Mind (ToM).[3]

Back in 2013, nearly all of the students entering Green were reading at about seven years below their grade level. Yet, four years later, after students began choosing their own texts and engaging in high levels of interpretive discourse, 83 percent of those same students passed all of the state reading and writing exams. How was this possible?

Theoretically, students who came to Green already had the skills to interpret, hypothesize, infer, and deduce. Since these abilities are acquired by all children at an early age through ordinary talk,[4] the kids at Green knew how to critically think, talk, and act for themselves. The students knew how to interpret the meaning of *what is said* and *what is meant*[5] in their own oral communities better than they could interpret what was written in a school text.

What accounted for this discrepancy?

DANTE: "SCHOOL READING KILLS MY VIBE"

When asked about his second-grade-level reading scores, Dante, a junior at Green, declared that, "School reading kills my vibe." He was not alone. Many students at Green expressed frustration and dismissiveness around reading.

In response to a culture of noncritical literacy programs, Green got rid of worksheets, generic essay writing, leveled-reading libraries, whole-class novels, and traditional reading-group instruction. Under the new approach, all students:

- choose which texts to read;
- read out loud together, chorally, in a cooperative reading group—in this case, in Cooperative Unison Reading®, where three simple rules require students to interpret text together for twenty minutes[6];

- lead the class as a group leader twice a year;
- breach, in the moment, and stop the group when they have questions or want to share a response while collectively reading a text;
- talk about their breach with others and work to resolve it together;
- are helpful, sharing, and caring toward others; and
- show leadership to help others follow school rules and practices.

What happened? Under this program, kids can think for themselves, and they can also pass the standardized tests and get into college. Most importantly, this approach protects the autonomy of the child and erodes that hatred of reading.

A PEDAGOGY FOR THINKING: ELIMINATE OPPRESSIVE TEACHING PRACTICES

If pursuing freedom of mind in the classroom is the goal, and the *elimination* of teaching practices that oppress a child's mind is the greatest obstacle, then getting the adults out of the way of the students' freedom to learn *how to learn* needs to be a focus for teachers and school leaders.

At Green, the following teacher-driven practices were eliminated:

- whole-class texts and teacher-mandated essay prompts and comprehension questions;
- teacher-determined essay writing or genre units of study in the standalone writing classes;
- teacher-generated essential questions;
- worksheets and graphic organizers; and
- PowerPoint lessons filled with facts and concepts to be stored and regurgitated in the form of a worksheet.

Instead, teachers did the following:

- coached students to cooperate and collectively interpret texts together;
- charged students with the responsibility to breach at the moment of confusion and talk about the breach together until they came to a common understanding of the text;
- required students to ask their own questions, thus determining their own teaching points;
- required students to pick their own texts to research the answers to their own questions (which, in content classes, mapped onto the standards or came from dissecting the standards);

- required students to write daily narrative summaries that were comprehensible to others; and
- asked students to write extended writing pieces each month.

When students begin to think for themselves, they are able to set goals, interpret, hypothesize, infer, and deduce the meaning of texts—and their reading levels go up. Moreover, they'll start to pass or excel on their high-stakes exams (with barely any test prep).

MICHAEL AND HIS TEXT CHOICE: ON CULTURAL RESPONSIVENESS

One day, during her first year as an assistant principal at Green, Maddie became frustrated while observing an inclusion class. A student, Michael, had wanted to read manga. Despite strongly expressing this preference, the teacher gave him an article on the Black Lives Matter movement to read.

This was not surprising. This is a tricky one because the teachers are trying really hard to be culturally relevant but doing it in a way that limits student agency. They are shooting themselves in the foot by imposing books on kids. That one action alone undermines the whole point of teaching critical literacy.

This new trend of the teacher choosing culturally relevant texts for kids, while well-intentioned, remains problematic for student intentionality. For one, this solution operates outside the learner's intention and control. The teacher remains the driver of learning and fails to give agency to the student. Secondly, it's about someone else's interpretation of what the student's culture is and doesn't teach children how to advocate for their own identity and selfhood.

Culturally responsive theories come from a good place, but their ideas not only operate outside the learners themselves, but also their ideas for reform fall on deaf ears in segregated, diverse schools. Teachers want to respect a student's culture so much that they end up making assumptions about a child's cultural identity and are still imposing the texts that the kids must read. Essentially, the teachers are trading out the whitewashed (pun intended!), Eurocentric titles for what teachers might think are more relevant for the children.

These teachers have yet again found another reason to limit student text choices. It's important to expose students to as many genres and topics as possible, but educators must stop telling a student to read about Bob Marley just because the student is from Jamaica or the Caribbean, or that they should read *The Land* or texts about basketball or President Barack Obama merely because they are African American.

Was this teacher trying to fill what she saw as a gap in the child's learning and experience? Was she trying to be culturally sensitive to the student? Whatever her motivation, he wanted to read manga. The teacher ignored the student's decision-making potential by failing to begin with the child's intentions and then determining how manga might or might not fit into his reading goals.

A lot of thought processes go into choosing a text to read. Why is choosing a text to read hard? It requires students to think about their own thinking. It forces students to ask what is on their mind before they choose a text: *What questions do I have? What do I want to learn or experience through reading? What goals do I want to achieve? What standards do I have to know? What do I like? What interests me? What do I care about? What do other people think about the issues I care about?*

Teaching students how to choose their own texts forces students to think about what is on their mind and what their own preferences and beliefs are. And, if nothing is on their mind, it forces students, at the very least, to explore the Internet a little, to see what topics pique their interest.

Students choosing their own texts to read in school is fundamental to them assuming their own unique identities. Maybe the teacher thought Michael should read an article on Black Lives Matter because she perceived it as a gap in his learning or experience. For whatever reason, she imposed her version of his cultural values on him by giving him a text to read.

When Michael is finished with manga, he may want to read about Black Lives Matter because that is what he might truly want to pursue next. Or he might want to pursue questions he has about Japanese internment camps during World War II because he is intrigued about how people make decisions during wartime. He might switch gears in two weeks and want to read more about cloning for one of his biology standards or because cloning interests him and answers some questions he has about God and the moral universe. But, for now, he wants to read manga.

TEACHING CRITICAL LITERACY

MaryAnne (name changed) taught at Green for six years. She talks about how educators think and apply critical literacy:

> In critical literacy, people try to understand the need for people to learn perspective and bias, and there are different people who decide what people get to learn, but I don't think it is being addressed in a way that starts again from the students and, ultimately, from what the students need. There are also teachers who say, "Kids should be reading books and articles about their culture, and so I am going to require that they read it because they need it to be successful in life." That's always the pushback.

> This also connects to what you were saying about being culturally responsive. We have to look at what the movement around culturally responsive education was rising up in response to and how it should require teachers to be continually responsive by allowing students to determine the focus of attention. It is problematic when teachers design curriculum ignoring who their students are or, worse, undermining and not giving value to their stories and identities in favor of the dominant identities and stories.
> Expose kids as much as possible and enable kids to know what is out there and so that way they can make certain decisions. And to say, "OK, we are going to read this text because I want to show you this." But it should be like genre exposure, and you want to expose kids to as many texts as possible to know how things get expressed in writing, and the same can happen in reading. Here are different perspectives on a topic in reading, and there are different types of texts that you might choose to do. It doesn't become a situation to tell a student to read a certain thing.

FREEDOM OF MIND: LET STUDENTS CHOOSE TOPICS AND TEXTS

For teachers, this is probably the most difficult aspect of a student-driven approach: teachers have a hard time giving up the power to choose what texts children should read. This is understandable, but it's necessary that they do so. When a teacher chooses the text, the teacher continues to hold the power over a child's mind. When students learn how to choose their own texts, they bring their personality and culture into that choice. Kids must learn how to choose their own texts based on their own questions, curiosities, goals, and desires as part of their own "becoming."

The following list illustrates the "critical identity revolution" that happens in a classroom when students can choose their own topics and texts to interpret with others. The students' unique cultural identities and interests are on full display in the lists below in table 4.1.

This list stands in stark contrast to the single, one-identity-driven topic text (i.e., Black Lives Matter) chosen by a teacher for a student to read. The topics on this list come from just three classrooms in the month of December. Who could have predicted students would have chosen such a wide range and depth of topics, genres, text complexity, and perspectives if given the freedom and tools to do so? The titles provide merely a small snapshot of how students choosing their own texts to read in schools should be a basic human right in culturally responsive schools to allow students to secure their own unique identity, their own epistemological and ontological stance in the world.

In this dialogue with the principal, an English Language Arts teacher, Kate, describes what it is like to follow the student's intentions in reading

Where to Begin. A small book about your power to create big change in our world
"We Miss: Why did 'iCarly' End? Answers to This and Your Other Burning Questions"
Time. "Inside the Record-Breaking Rise of Lil Nas X"
New York Times. Should Blowouts Be Allowed in Youth Sports
Gotham: "New TV Show Imagines the City Before Batman"
New York Times: Popeyes Sandwich Strikes a Chord for African-Americans
"Meet the cannibal who became a hero in Japan"
The Bridge of Sighs-Poem by Thomas Hodd
BBC: "Bolivia Mayor has hair forcibly cut by crowd of protesters"
Brothers of The Gun: A Memoir of The Syrian War
Burn It Down: Women Writing About Anger
City of Inmates: Conquest, Rebellion, and the Rise of Human Gaging in Los Angeles, 1171-1965
Dear Girls
The Tell-Tale Heart
"What Happens After Death?"
"Rape in The Military"
"Black Girls Must Die Exhausted"
"Heaven or Hell"
"Unsolved Murders"
"The Central Park Five"
"A Good Man Is Hard to Find"
"What Causes Some People to Be Overly Attached to Their Pets?"
"Filling Out College Applications"
"Can Biology Class Reduce Racism?" by Amy Harmon NYTimes
"You Mean You Don't Weep at the Nail Salon?" by Elizabeth Acevedo Poetry Foundation
How to Be an Anti-Racist
The Great Pretender
Solito, Solita
Kicks: Great American Story of Sneakers
Edison
Basketball A Love Story
American Prison: A Reporter's Undercover Journey into The Business Of Punishment

and how, even though it's hard giving up the power to direct learning or ask the questions and choose the texts, she wouldn't change it for anything.

Kate: The opposite of dominating or just talking at the kids isn't just to shut up—or maybe the opposite is—but the solution or the role of the teacher that the student-driven format intends is a kind of presence and a responsiveness to students that I think, for me, is the most exciting and intellectually engaging; it's my favorite part of my job and day, every day. It requires a kind of presence and an ability to constantly be able to shift *my* perspective. How incredible is it that that's my job, right? That's amazing. I don't just stand up in front of a group of kids and say a packaged thing and have them say it back to me. I must be this fully present human being all the time. It's so amazing. It really, that's why I stay. There are a lot of reasons why I stay, but that part is why it is still exciting to me. I am always learning.

Principal: Why?

K: Because it's real human interaction. Because of my own vulnerability and my own . . . again, my work isn't to come up with something brilliant to say, or not brilliant to say, about what to think about a text and stand in front of an English classroom and say, "Here is what Hamlet means when he says A, B or C." My job is to listen deeply to, A, what they care about reading, and then, B, to what they wonder about, question, want to know more about, and think about what they are reading, and to respond to that and to support them in answering those questions; not by themselves, in isolation by themselves, but to answer them collectively, to answer them with my support to understand the resources that are available to unwater those questions. It is so much richer; it is so much, and it is more of a real way of learning. I think you see they're human beings. They are not robots.

Principal: Do you think it takes the kids to where you would have taken them had you just stood there with your teacher-directed, planned lesson? Do the kids go where you wanted to take them in the book or in the piece?

K: No, rarely. I think it takes them to places that surprise me, and I think that is what is exciting about it, that it is surprising.

Principal: Sometimes it's slow. Sometimes the first sentence takes them two days, and they can't get past the title sometimes or the picture or the caption. So, people get frustrated with that.

K: Yeah, I mean, I get frustrated with that, but I think I trust that if they are asking the questions then they are going to understand the answer. If I am asking the questions, they are not going to care about the answer so much. I think making sure that they are aware of their reading ability, and that they understand and inhabit their own data and make choices accordingly, that they are always pushing more and more complex texts is really important. This is always something we are strengthening.

Teachers will have no idea what students are truly interested in pursuing or capable of achieving if they are not allowed to think about and act on their own desires, thoughts, and intentions for reading. Text choices like the varied titles mentioned here, and a student's ability to interpret texts with others, goes to the heart of liberating the child's mind in school, as it requires the child to think about how reading can help shape one's unique identity and beliefs.

In the following exchange, the students who spoke earlier in this chapter, including another student, Sira, discuss how this new learning approach felt to them:

Principal: Do you think you'd be better off reading by yourself?

Sira: No, to be honest.

Naya: No, I don't think I understand it reading by myself. I can understand some things, but to understand the whole idea of the piece, no. When you are with your Unison Reading group, you are understanding other people's thoughts, their opinions, and they argue their own opinion, and they can even give you some facts if they know something else about the topic. When I first came here, I did not know how to read and be able to process my own thinking by myself. So, when I came here, and I had to work with other people, and it was very healthy. It benefited me so much so in a way that now I can read better by myself. I can feed off of their thinking and become more of a literate person.

Sira: When I came to Green Careers, I didn't know how to work with other people because I was so used to learning by myself. So, being here taught me how to open up more and work with other people. A great learning experience to work with other people just like me. And we are all graduating on time! *[Everyone cheers]*

Johancarla: At first, I was confused . . . I didn't think that [this school] would benefit me in any way. But, eventually, I learned that I could learn from other people as well as bounce ideas off of other people. Overall, Learning Cultures®[7] has helped me, especially outside of school life, because before, I could not communicate effectively with other people.

Often, children have been so thoroughly indoctrinated in oppressive educational approaches that they struggle to adjust to this newfound freedom. As Paulo Freire writes, "The oppressed are fearful of freedom." The students at Green (like Jayden, who appeared earlier in this chapter), initially unused to having freedom ingrained across their curriculum and pedagogical approach, actively resisted it.

Naya, Sira, Sallie Mae, and Johancarla also initially resisted freedom, but they gave it a chance, and eventually, they embraced it, as did most of the students. They liked being in control of their own mental capacities and learning how to think and communicate their thoughts effectively.

NOTES

1. Paulo Freire, *Pedagogy of the Oppressed* (New York: Herder and Herder, 1972), 77.
2. David R. Olson, *The Mind on Paper: Reading, Consciousness and Rationality* (Cambridge, UK: Cambridge University Press, 2016), 136.

3. "In Western cultures, at least, we tend to think of such understandings as an understanding of the mind. Indeed, children are said to have a 'theory of mind' [ToM] if they can use ascriptions of beliefs and desires as means of interpreting or explaining the sayings and actions of themselves or others." From David R. Olson, *The World on Paper: The Conceptual and Cognitive Implications of Writing and Reading* (Cambridge, UK: Cambridge University Press, 1996), 250.

4. "The concepts *think, know, mean,* as well as simple modal verbs *might be, could be, must be* are part of the oral competence of very young children." From Olson, *The World on Paper*, 281.

5. "The say–mean distinction is fundamental to all interpretation in that it allows the independent specification of the meaning in the language—what is said—and of the communicative intention of the speaker—what is meant." From Olson, *The World on Paper*, 130.

6. 1. Read out loud *in sync* together so you can hear each other. 2. *Breach* the group when you have a question or something to say and talk about it together until the group resolves the breach. 3. *Be promotive* and helpful to group members. Cynthia McCallister, *Unison Reading: Social Inclusive Group Instruction for Equity and Achievement* (New York: Corwin Press, 2011), 4.

7. Cynthia McCallister, 2018, https://cynthiamccallister.com/.

Chapter Five

Speak

David R. Olson has noted that "Language is less a tool than the very medium of thinking."[1] *This assertion undergirds the emphasis of this book on student voice. The central place of communication and thinking is illustrated by the concept of "breaching," by which students are encouraged to pause during group reading to question and reflect on what they are reading. Breaching is commonly used during Cooperative Unison Reading®,*[2] *one of the primary learning formats employed at Green. Every class includes Unison Reading, during which student leaders post short, whole texts, and every student chooses one of those texts to read in a group. Each group reads the chosen text aloud together. Breaching and respect and support for one another are expected.*

Even intractable, seemingly hopeless students have found their voices through the practice of Cooperative Unison Reading®,[3] *as the example of Kyle that will follow shows. After hundreds of conferences, as well as nearly two years of refusing to settle down and join any reading groups, Kyle eventually quietly chose to join a reading group one day and began contributing on a regular basis. Kyle's case illustrates how, when staff and students create a helpful community and work to pull students into the group, instead of pushing them out of the group, even the most fringe students will often come to the table by choice.*

In a more traditional academic setting, teachers would be encouraged to "protect" a low-performing student like Kyle from the embarrassment of exposure to and interaction with other students. Separating or pulling students out into tiered classrooms, or even putting students into leveled-ability groups within the classroom, inadvertently fosters an exclusionary culture in schools.

Such a practice also undermines the development of critical literacy skills and the honing of the "linguistic turn,"[4] *which is key to developing an ability to read texts critically and analytically. This shift from reading texts at face value and not questioning or interrogating the author's words, to teaching students that texts can and should be dissected and discussed, is the difference between teaching "learning to read so students can read to learn" and teaching critical literacy.*

Given the importance of critical literacy, it makes sense to design curricula so that children spend the maximum amount of time actively speaking in an interpretive, text-focused community. The closing examples in this chapter, in which the reader sees Jeanne's class in action during two Unison Reading groups, shows how this approach fosters critical thinking, development of literacy skills, and interpersonal relationships.

LIBERATE STUDENT VOICES AND LIBERATE THINKING

In his book *The Mind on Paper*, David Olson disputes Dewey's claim that language is merely a tool to mediate learning. Olson asserts that, rather than a mediator of the thinking process, language itself *is* the act of thinking. As he puts it, "Language is less a tool than the very medium of thinking." Olson cites Vygotsky's own studies that still ring true today to support his own claim about language and thinking, "aphasic patients, those who have lost the power of speech, also lose their ability to think and to plan (1986, p. 134), suggesting that thinking and speaking are much the same thing."[5]

"BREACH!"

Liberating the student voice at Green is how students began to be mindful and to think about thoughts—their own thoughts and the thoughts of others. At Green, the student voice is held in high esteem and recognized as the very act of thinking. As Sira, a student at Green, notes, "Using our voice is very important. When kids first come to this school, they don't realize they have a voice and they can use it. After a while, they can talk to students and peers, and they learn that they have a say."

Since liberating student voice is a fundamental part of a pedagogy of freedom, it became a rule for everyone "to breach" at the school. Breaching is when a student (or any person, really) realizes that they have a confusion or information to share and, at the moment of that realization, says something to someone else about it. A breach is an intentional state. Students breach when they make their internal mental states (e.g., confusion, thoughts, opinions, beliefs, etc.) conscious and public to others, who are the object of student's focus and attention. For example, when a student is unclear about the meaning of a word, phrase, or passage being read, or has additional information to share on the topic of the passage, he or she breaches.[6]

Breaching keeps students from drowning in confusion. One former student describes it this way: "Breaching is about rising up and catching your breath." Breaching gives control over their own minds back to students. At the moment of breaching, students realize they are straddling the "Zone of

Proximal Development" or "no-man's-land"[7] of learning; they breach to make their disjunctures conscious and to acquire new knowledge. Learning how to liberate the voice through breaching is fundamental to students' ability to use language as a medium for thinking.

LIBERATING VOICE (AND MIND) IN COOPERATIVE UNISON READING®

Cooperative Unison Reading®[8] is a forceful learning format—and also the hardest one to implement. At first, students resist the freedoms inherent in Cooperative Unison Reading®.[9] Once the students liberate their voices and minds in Unison Reading by breaching and making their thinking public, they begin to interpret meaning together. Invariably, their test scores also rise, and then students value this learning approach immensely.

For twenty minutes a day, all classrooms at Green provide opportunities for students to talk and think about texts in Cooperative Unison Reading®.[10] In every class, five group leaders each post on the wall for everyone to see a short text based on their own interests that they believe might also appeal to their classmates. Students chose one of five groups, each of which is devoted to reading one of the leader-chosen texts. Each group reads together for two weeks, following some basic rules:

1. Read in sync so that you can hear others and others can hear you.
2. Breach the group when you have a question or something to say, and talk about it until the group comes to a common understanding of what the breach means and can close the breach. In other words, when they know they know it and can decide it's time to move on.
3. Be promotive to others.

After two weeks, the cycle repeats with a new group leader who chooses a new text, and students select new groups.

At first, most students hated to read in their Unison Reading groups. It's not easy! In Unison Reading, students have to develop skills to coordinate their own thinking, speaking, and actions with others by:

- reading the text out loud, in sync, and listening intently to determine the author's intent and meaning;
- staying alert to their own internal mental states and recognizing when they, or someone else, might have a question or something to say;
- breaching and stopping their group at the moment to make their own thoughts and reactions conscious and public;

- talking about what the author is saying and what the author means while considering each other's and their own thoughts, too; and
- closing the breach by making sure the group has a shared understanding of what the author's words mean on the page (i.e., the author's intention) before moving on.

KYLE: LIBERATING STUDENT VOICES TO BRING STUDENTS BACK INTO THE GROUP

Every school has students like Kyle. Kyle's behavior got in the way of his learning, and the learning of others, in every classroom. On a daily basis, a familiar routine occurred. He wandered around from table to table and talked loudly: "Where is my notebook? I can't find my notebook!" He would never sit down at a Unison Reading table, ever. He made many excuses, but he would not sit down to read, write, or do anything. Every system teachers put into place to help him didn't work.

The students in his Unison Reading groups asked him to sit down to read together with them. Students offered him paper and their own notebooks. The classroom teachers called the on-call teacher so that they could conduct a behavior or learning conference with him. But Kyle never kept the promises he made in teacher conferences.

In Kyle's first year at Green, teachers conducted hundreds of classroom behavior and learning conferences with him, and the other students kept inviting him to read in groups. No one gave up, but Kyle's behavior did not improve that first year.

By the end of Kyle's second year, his behavior had improved, but he still refused to sit down at the table with others. At the end of his sophomore year, the principal began to think it might actually be time for Kyle to transfer to another school because even though his behavior was better, and he had passed one Regents exam in January, she was worried he still wouldn't have time to complete all of his requirements for graduation from Green.

And then, seemingly out of nowhere, Kyle pulled a seat up to the table. Kyle chose a text he wanted to read, sat down with a group, breached, and talked about meaning. It was undramatic and quiet. And eventually, Kyle ended up graduating on time.

During the interviews for this book, many teachers brought up Kyle. His story illustrates how, when staff and students create a helpful community and work to pull students into the group, instead of pushing them out of the group, even the most fringe students will often eventually come to the table by choice.

Math teacher Dan Grenell gives a really good explanation as to why he thinks Kyle, and so many others like him, finally found his voice and joined his Unison Reading table: "Everyone is lifted in Unison Reading [UR]. Everyone. With every experience in UR, everyone gets better at it—even the kid who refuses to sit at the table that eventually does sit at the table, and then he doesn't breach, but he listens. Think about Kyle. He ended up sitting at the table. He joined after wandering the room for a year and not sitting down. He slowly participated by listening in, and then he started to take part and breach, and then have conversations."

Kyle did not just sit down one day randomly; rather, he was consistently included in a group, so that, eventually, he wanted to belong and change his behaviors to engage with the group. Ultimately, Dan attributes rule #3 of Union Reading ("Be Promotive") as the reason why so many students like Kyle finally join in: "That is why rule # 3—be promotive to the group—is one of the three rules and important to teach into. There are things that you, as a teacher, need to do when you are in a teacher-led UR group, and the thing to do is to really reinforce rule 3. We talk a lot about rule 2—breach and talk—but kids have a lot of anxiety around whether they are smart or whether they are dumb or whether they think of themselves as smart. And that is a big thing that keeps Kyle back. He is worried he will say something where others will think he is dumb. Kyle was best in my class this year when he was with Ronnie, Sallie Mae, and Rosalynn."

Here, the principal interjected with "Really?"

Dan continued, "*Yes*, because those four kids, you would look at them and say they should not be near each other. But, they really petitioned for it, and when they were together, they didn't feel self-conscious. These were the people they trusted, and so it was, like, 'I am OK breaching around them.' Rosalynn got switched out, but when they were together, they were functional. I didn't think it was going to work. But it worked because there was a lot of trust; they were promotive, and so, they could breach.

"The whole idea of drawing all kids in, like the students that really do Unison Reading and use it for learning, helps everyone improve. There is a criticism that the higher kids—higher skilled in certain areas, that is—might do better in it. They are more social or whatever the reasons are. But that's not the case. Kids who are shy or insecure even have a good time with it. But I think that everyone's level is lifted through rule #3—be promotive—like you always said."

Dan posits that the group that Kyle was in was less about level than it was about creating a safe space where he had social support. His success wasn't because there was a mix of high- and low-level readers. His peers lobbied to be together because they all knew they wouldn't be labeled as "dumb" in their group. Unison Reading, and rule #3 especially, pull kids in because they help students create a safe space to learn, which they come to advocate for and value.

When students start to use their voices and advocate for each other, it can push against all of the teacher's control instincts. If Dan had relied too heavily on his initial reflexive instincts, and not allowed these students to be together, he would have missed this opportunity for the kids to create their own safe learning environment and, in turn, absorb the school's most fringe student. Teachers can't fully know what will make students feel comfortable and make them want to participate in a conversation around their learning. It's important for teachers to empower students to advocate for a safe learning space and then hold them responsible for learning in it.

In situations like this, educators may think that students like Kyle would be embarrassed if they have to engage with students working at higher levels, so they might be tempted to keep students like Kyle out of groups to "protect" him. Teachers might also think that a child such as Kyle can't possibly learn unless the teacher directly teaches into the student's skills, needs, and deficits. For these reasons, students such as Kyle get pulled out of the group to work with a specialized teacher in a small classroom with other students like themselves.

Separating or pulling students out into tiered classrooms, or even putting students into leveled-ability groups within the classroom, is a clinical, targeted, child-centered response to intervention, and as a side-effect, it fosters an exclusionary culture in schools. As Chris Sedita, the Building Science teacher at Green, boldly put it, "Where does the removed kid go? Not into another rich learning environment. It's even worse than segregation; removing a student is not even 'separate, but equal,' it's just separate. It harkens back to when slaves were denied education. It's validating the fundamentals of slavery with every new generation. Slavery . . . Jim Crow . . . prison. School has been a cog in this wheel since the start. It's time to destroy it."

It wasn't easy, but Green teachers created an environment that empowered students to advocate for other students to join in the groups and work and learn together. Everyone worked together to help Kyle feel safe enough to pull up his chair to the Unison Reading table and confidently use his voice to breach and talk. Kyle was never kicked out, pulled out, or excluded. The students were the ones who eventually empowered Kyle to join in and learn.

THE LINGUISTIC TURN: LITERACY IS BEING ABLE TO TALK ABOUT THINKING AND KNOWING

Educators will often say, "Children first learn to read, and then read to learn." Literacy is more than just learning to read or reading to learn or figuring out what something means. People who are critically literate have the language and concepts available to be able to speak about what they know, think, or believe; what other people know, think and believe; and the beliefs and intentions of the author.[11]

Dan brings up some important insights into literacy and the discrepancy between this idea of traditional reading instruction and becoming critically literate, even in another discipline such as math.

"The misconception is that math is about figuring out the right answers and then internalizing it, and that is just not the case. There are a hundred different ways to view something, and you know, I have heard a lot of them, but there are still times when kids still say, 'That's new to me' and 'I never thought of it that way.' And, you know, certainly, if you are learning something for the first time, the other things that people have to say are vital. They are vital for you to have a rich understanding of the subject. You can have a core understanding of something with your own perspective or a rich understanding with a lot of other people's perspectives. And, just like learning how to engage with different types of texts—I still see kids sitting with a textbook, and some kid will say, 'Did you guys look at the thing on the side?' You know, the sidebar, and everyone will go and look at that. The experience is enriched, and it is more fun to be doing things with other people."

Olson refers to a "literate" person as someone who can think and speak about texts using the "linguistic turn." He explains the linguistic turn as "the shift in emphasis on the discussion of whiteness of snow to the discussion of the truth of 'snow is white.'" The linguistic turn is where "this discourse is designed to facilitate the judgment of *truth* and *validity*."[12] This shift from reading texts at face value and not questioning or interrogating the author's words, to teaching students that texts can and should be dissected, questioned, discussed and judged, is the difference between teaching "learning to read so students can read to learn" and teaching critical literacy.

Importantly, Olson adds more about the importance of oral discourse patterns and literate thought: "Literate thought can be, indeed is to some degree, embedded in the oral discourse of a literate society. We can talk of conjectures just as well as read and write about them. Literate thought is not restricted to the medium of writing, even if writing and reading were critical in their evolution. The concepts of *think, know, mean*, as well as simple modal verbs *might be, could be, must be* are part of the oral competence of very young children." The practice of literate thinking and critical reading are the same things. "There is no gap between the 'two cultures.'"[13]

Vygotsky discusses how children learn socially, and he suggests that what people learn from their experiences in the social sphere are internalized. "Vygotsky links the social and the personal by suggesting that the learner first practices an activity such as speaking with another person, an interpersonal function, that later becomes an intrapersonal function, used later for private thinking. So, for example, promises made to one can become promises made by one."[14]

Based on these accepted definitions of critical thinking and literacy, it makes sense to design curricula so that children spend the maximum amount of time actively speaking in an interpretive, text-focused community and spend minimal time in "reading to learn" activities, which is what most educators consider the primary reading activity after third grade. Educators often refer to the need to teach children how to read critically or "be critical readers," but the choice of pedagogical models often directly conflicts with the definition of critical literacy.

If educators knew what critical reading and literacy really meant, principals and teachers would not allow content memorization, didactic teaching, worksheets, scripted programs, units of study, or other reductionist reading programs to dominate the learning minutes in school.

JEANNE-MARIE ZONNEVELD'S ENGLISH LANGUAGE ARTS CLASS DOING THE LINGUISTIC TURN

Bearing in mind the concept of the "linguistic turn,"[15] students should be going much deeper than just "reading to learn" for content in school reading communities. The focus instead should be on developing their "metalanguage" for talking about reading and their "thinking about knowing."[16]

In the following two examples, students in Jeanne-Marie Zonneveld's class do the linguistic turn naturally as if it were a dance sequence. They have a complete repertoire of language for speaking about and judging the validity of the author's statements. In these two examples, students grapple with the propositions "sleeping enough will make you live longer," and "Is Google making us stupid?"

The text chosen was "Oversleeping: The Effects and Health Risks of Sleeping Too Much" by Rosie Osmun. Before beginning, the students talk about why the group leader chose the text. This conversation created the group intention for reading it.

BR: Who picked the text?

CC: I did.

BR: So . . . what is it?

CC: It's about oversleeping.

JV: Why did you pick it?

CC: I don't know.

JZ: This is awkward because I watched you explain this text to Farid.

CC: Oh, yeah. [*laughs*] OK, OK, it was because I wanted to know more about oversleeping. We were arguing about it.

JV: Do you oversleep?

CC: No.

BR: Yooo, what are you arguing about?

JV: He never said he was arguing that sleeping too much was good.

BR: Oh, yeah.

CC: I don't think oversleeping is bad, but I think this article will say it is because I looked at it already.

BR: So let's read.

They read it out loud, unfolding the words in sync so that their minds keep track of the author's meaning together. One student stops the group to check in on a student who appears to have a "breach face." She calls out another student who moves in a way that is not promotive.

BR: Yo.

CC: Do you have a breach?

BR: No.

JZ: Are you sure? You have breach face. [*Group laughs*]

JV: CC was moving awkwardly, on purpose.

JZ: Let's call him out.

BR: Can you not move your body so weirdly?

CC: I wasn't!

MG: Yes, you were. You were dabbing him.

CC: OK, OK, I'm sorry.

With the whole group poised and ready, they begin to read in sync until one student breaches and says, "What are we considering oversleeping?" With this question, the students start to play with the linguistic turn and interrogate the author's and their own beliefs about oversleeping. They consider each other's thoughts, talk about what they already know about sleeping, and consider some of the nuances of their breach. These turns of conversation lead them to ask more questions (i.e., how much is too little sleep?), and then they go back into the text.

JV: What are we considering oversleeping?

BR: Average sleep is seven to nine hours, it says, so I guess more.

CC: My mom told me eight.

JV: Do you sleep that much?

MG: It depends; you know, the day, what's going on . . .

BR: And when I go to sleep, the latest I go to bed is three in the morning.

JV: There are times when I just take a quick nap and wake up and head to school.

BR: I've done that.

CC: Same.

JV: If I'm doing the math correctly, I get about five hours of sleep.

MG: So how bad is that?

CC: Let's keep reading.

The students breach because one student loses track of meaning and needs to stop to think. For the group to keep track of meaning and stay coordinated, the group rereads together.

JZ: Breach.

BR: What happened?

JZ: I think we're thinking.

CC: Wait, I needed to reread.

JZ: Take us with you. [*Group rereads*]

Once they reread in sync, a student has another breach, and this time the breach is a question about what the author means by oversleeping.

BR: So, if you get more sleep than that, it's bad?

JV: Apparently; do we continue?

CC: Yeah, because I still don't get it.

They read on and breach on the word "longevity."

JV: Wait, well, what does "longevity" mean?

CC: I don't know what that means.

JZ: MG, I see you doing something.

MG: I'm rereading.

JZ: Bring us with you. [*Group rereads*]

Students reread and think about what they know and decide they still don't know what the author meant by "longevity," make some guesses, but then decide to look it up.

JV: It sounds positive, you know?

MG: Maybe a long time?

CC: I think it means you live longer.

BR: Did you look that up?

MG: Should I look it up?

CC: Sure, do that. [*MG Googles on laptop*]

MG: He's right.

The students consider what the author meant by "longevity," and the group talks about how they know what "longevity" means.

JV: OK, what is the sentence saying?

MG: Sleeping will make you live longer?

BR: I think sleeping seven hours a night makes you live longer, if you look at the whole sentence.

JV: I agree.

All the students in this group, two with IEP's and low reading levels and two with above-average reading levels, could do the linguistic turn. This is not easy. First of all, students selected their own text and could state the reason why they selected it. ("I wanted to know more about oversleeping. We were arguing about it.") They read it together out loud so their attention could be in sync. This enables students to think about their own thinking and bring it into consciousness to be discussed with others.

Next, they breached ("What are we considering oversleeping?"). With this question, the students started to play with the linguistic turn and interpret what the author actually meant to say to the reader about oversleeping ("Average sleep is seven to nine hours, it says, so I guess more"). They thought about their own and each others' thinking about this and breached again on the word "longevity," looked it up, and then put their understanding of the definition back into the author's sentence to consider if the dictionary definition aligned with the way the author intended to use the word. Then they all agreed on a common understanding.

The next example shows a group reading an article from *The Atlantic*, "Is Google Making Us Stupid? What the Internet Is Doing to Our Brains." The text starts with a painting of a police officer standing next to his police car with the words "Internet Patrol" blazoned across the trunk. The police officer is standing in front of the police car writing a ticket to a man, who is on the road carrying only a red book in his hand (with no personal car in sight), next to a sign that says "MINIMUM SPEED 186 292 387 MPS."

Teacher: What made you choose this?

J: It looked interesting.

S: I chose this because it's the opposite of what the Internet is supposed to do—it's supposed to help make you smart.

G: Like you said, it's supposed to help you understand, but I think it's saying it's making people lazy.

J: We depend on Google too much.

E: I want to know why the author makes such a bold statement in the title—what's he saying?

G: We'd have to read.

Teacher: So how do we read this? How do we approach this?

G: Read it seriously.

E: The author is trying to teach us why Google is making us dumb, so we should find out what he's saying.

J: We should start at the title. [*Group reads*]

Teacher: Breach—we broke a rule.

From the start, the students decide to analyze the genre features in the painting.

J: Sorry, I was looking at the picture. What is the sign saying?

G: "Internet Patrol."

J: I feel like it's supposed to make us think.

E: It reminds me of a political cartoon.

J: Why is he stopping the guy? "Internet Patrol" means what?

G: How does this tie to making us stupid?

E: Yeah, I don't get if it's saying that the Internet stops us, like J said.

The student "J" breaches the group to discuss the author's supposition, "Is Google making us stupid?" The student initially breaches the group when he looks at the picture: "Sorry—I was looking at the picture—what is the sign saying?" Then, attempting to understand what "Internet Patrol" means, J says, "I feel like it's supposed to make us think." In a third turn of conversation, J explicitly asks about the validity of the author's statement: "How does this tie to making us stupid?"

What is powerful about these two examples is that, in Unison Reading, students often choose texts that challenge their own assumptions or biases, which makes them want to breach and talk about provocative ideas together. The linguistic turn happens all the time in classrooms at Green. When students focus on the validity of ideas and concepts, and their own beliefs, it's more empowering than just reading a text for understanding and only considering the author's point of view. When a pedagogy focuses on teaching students how to liberate their voices, it liberates their thinking—and students come to value this time spent critically reading together.

NOTES

1. David R. Olson, *The Mind on Paper: Reading, Consciousness and Rationality* (Cambridge, UK: Cambridge University Press, 2016), 54.
2. Cynthia McCallister, *Unison Reading: Socially Inclusive Group Instruction for Equity and Achievement* (New York: Corwin Press, 2011), 5–6.
3. Ibid.
4. Olson, *The Mind on Paper*.
5. Olson, *The Mind on Paper*, 53–54.
6. McCallister writes "Breaches essentially break open the reading process to create spaces or gaps for collective reasoning and speculation to occur. When a question or comment is brought to the group, children have an opportunity to think referentially." McCallister, *Unison Reading*, 5.
7. The Zone of Proximal Development is "the distance between the actual developmental level as determined by independent problem solving and the level of potential development as determined through problem solving under adult guidance or in collaboration with more capable peers." From L. S. Vygotsky, *Mind in Society: The Development of Higher Psychological Processes* (Cambridge, MA: Harvard University Press, 1978), 214.
8. McCallister, *Unison Reading*, 70–72.
9. Ibid.
10. Ibid.
11. "Literate adults capable of thinking about language have learned a metalanguage that allows them to beware of unacknowledged assumptions, hidden premises, and invalid inferences, especially when they occur in reading and writing texts. Competence with ordinary language provides one with reasons, but specific metalinguistic distinctions are required to see reasons as reasons and to determine their status in a logical argument. Literacy education achieves its fuller significance when it accepts this larger mandate and the concept of mind will become more adequate when it acknowledges the role of literacy and education in its development." From Olson, *The Mind on Paper*, 242–43.
12. Olson, *The Mind on Paper*, 135–36.
13. David R. Olson, *The World on Paper: The Conceptual and Cognitive Implications of Writing and Reading* (Cambridge, UK: Cambridge University Press, 1994), 281.
14. Olson, *The Mind on Paper*, 53.
15. Olson, *The Mind on Paper*.
16. Olson, *The Mind on Paper*, 136.

Chapter Six

Act

Teachers can best support students' freedom and autonomy by getting out of their way. Rather than top-down instruction, worksheets, and rote memorization, teachers should provide students with the resources they need to find solutions themselves to questions of their own choosing.

But a transition toward this kind of approach is not easy for educators or students—especially in a struggling school where kids are failing to pass classes and graduate. Giving up teacher control can seem counterintuitive and counterproductive. But Sugata Mitra's "Hole in the Wall Experiment" suggests the power of self-initiated education. Mitra placed a computer with Internet access into the side of a wall in a remote village in India, and over time, children taught themselves and each other how to use it. Mitra calls this Minimally Invasive Education (MIE).

At Green, three protocols were put in place to solidify the practice of student-led learning: Learning Conference, Responsibility Teams, and Writing Share.

The Learning Conference is a one-on-one meeting during which the student directs the conversation and the teacher offers support and suggestions but not answers or directives. Teachers focus on coaching students to plan their short-and long-term goals and how best to achieve them.

Responsibility Teams are groups of students who are given a problem, as well as the proper resources for solving it, after which the teacher steps back to let the students figure it out among themselves. Although this type of problem-solving can be slow going, especially at first, eventually, the students at Green embraced it and took responsibility for their own learning.

During the Writing Share, students display their written work, which has been composed in a genre of their own choosing, before their classmates. The writer receives extensive public feedback and then revises the piece accordingly. Over time, students learn how to critically read texts and judge whether the author applied the genre features in a way that best served his or her intention.

> *David R. Olson states the following: "Acting intentionally is what grants autonomy and freedom to the doer; one is free to the extent that one's own actions are intentional, in one's own control, rather than caused, forced, or prescribed by another . . . it is this autonomy that allows the formation of unique personal identity, a self."*[1]

Once students enter school, many factors inhibit their ability to act intentionally. An emphasis on worksheets, low expectations, and overly bureaucratic teaching processes inside the classroom all inhibit a student's freedom to act and learn independently and collaboratively.

Students benefit when teachers get out of the way in school and let students' neurons do more of their firing. To that end, all of the adults' actions at Green revolved around student intentions. MaryAnne, a former teacher at Green, describes how she saw her role as a teacher change when she began teaching into, and in support of, students' intentions:

> You start with the kids' strengths as opposed to their deficits. When you start with the deficits, then you are tempted to say, "It's so much easier if I just give the information to the students, let me just stand here and teach it." But, if you start with what the kids can do right now and then follow into that with a strategy, then you can have kids take ownership over their learning in a way that is feasible. Otherwise, people try to bring about independence where there is no structure to it, which can be haphazard.

Empowering students requires a shift in the classroom power dynamic. When students are empowered, they initiate, direct, and control their own actions and the teacher follows into their intentional acts. To do this effectively, teachers must learn how to start with the student's strengths. Starting with student strengths requires teachers to adopt the mindset that students must initiate and direct their own actions. At Green, shedding the students' *and* the teachers' dependence on teacher control and direction was one of the biggest hurdles to overcome.

TEACHING STUDENTS INDEPENDENCE: THE LEARNING CONFERENCE

A coaching protocol was necessary to help students learn how to function independently and outside of teacher direction. A student-driven classroom that adheres to the Five Principles of Freedom requires students to learn how to be self-directed and to use the resources available to them—communication, learning formats, resources, and other people—effectively.

The Learning Conference plays a key role in the development of student-led learning. It has two primary objectives: (1) to help students learn how to go from stuck to unstuck independent of the teacher; and (2) to coach students to plan their short- and long-term goals so that their daily actions help them achieve their long-term outcomes.

Students Sallie Mae, Naya, Sira, and Eric describe the Learning Conference protocol, and what it really meant to them to learn independently and in a self-led way:

Naya: Basically, you have a question or a challenge that you are facing and that is when you and the teacher walk through it—they will ask you first what do you understand, where do you get stuck at, like, what is your question that you're trying to solve, and then you both can walk through it together.

When you get over that hump and you try to figure out what the problem is, you have what you are going to do in the future next time you have a problem. You're gonna have a resolution basically as to what you can do moving forward. Or you can apply the same method as you used to solve it on your own.

Sallie Mae: I ask for one [a Learning Conference] every day. There is a Conference Sheet, so when Naya says you start with a breach, start with something that we don't know, and then they take us from something we do know, they ask us what do we know, then we have to state the unknown, something we don't know about the topic. And then the resolution, it says, "Resolve your breach relating what you don't know to what you do know." Your teacher might participate, but you should lead the discussion. And then they ask us the Takeaway. Like, what are you going to do in the future, what did you *get* from this conference? They want us to explain what we did, like the process. And then, it says the narrative. Retell your conference as a story. Yeah, I like that. Then the commitment.

The narrative is basically like what you did, how you did it, how you came to figure out your breaches.

Sira: I feel like a conference is like a phone call. You call up somebody, and you tell them your problem, and they either help you out or they don't. But, let's say we're having a conference with a teacher, and you tell them, "This is what I am working on, this is what I need help with," and the teacher gives you feedback, and it's how you use that feedback, and you either use it or not; you decide if it can be helpful or not.

Principal: Feedback for the future, not just that problem?

S: Yes.

Principal: What was it like for you to not be able to get an answer from the teachers? It wasn't like you could raise your hand throughout every class and get the answer, right?

SM: I struggled until I, one, started doing it by myself, and two, started to ask for help. Once I understand what I could do . . .

Eric: It got me mad because, like, you, the teacher, just tell me the answer. I figure it out later.

S: It was annoying because I felt like the teacher should be teaching us, but after a while, I was like, you know what, I am going to do it by myself because I felt like I will get a better understanding, and it stays in my head, and then I can teach others.

N: Yes, I think that is important. When you do things by yourself and you do your own research, it sticks more in your head, whereas you can tell me the answer, and I will write it down, but I will just forget it. Like, the teacher teaches you the process of thinking about it. We learn the whole process on how to answer that same question multiple ways versus the teacher telling us how to answer that question.

Principal: What do you mean "the whole process"?

N: When I say "process," for example, like in math, if I am doing something about systems of equations, and it's just that one problem on systems of equations, and the teacher would just tell me how to solve that one problem on systems of equations but not actually teach me to actually solve systems of equations. Whereas us, we are doing our own learning how to do multiple systems of equations. And we are not just learning how to solve that one problem—our learning is extended.

Giving feedback to students and coaching them on these independent learning processes can be tricky; people just don't like to hear feedback about their weaknesses. The Learning Conference protocol avoids these potential pitfalls because students lead the entire conference. Here is an example of a Learning Conference in math teacher Dan Grenell's classroom.

The teacher starts by asking the student about the question at hand, and the student responds:

Student: I am working on resolving my breach in my notebook: How do you find the median of a trapezoid?

The teacher asks the student to think about what she already knows about how to solve the challenge:

> **Student**: I know you have to make the largest side equal to the other side.
>
> **Teacher**: Where did you find this information?
>
> **Student**: Isaiah helped me. He told me that the mid-segment is the same as the top and bottom.
>
> **Teacher**: He gave you some misinformation.

The teacher identifies her confusion and coaches the student to think more about what she already knows to help her resolve her challenge. The student tells the teacher that she tried to search for her topic in the textbook, but she couldn't find it, so she asked Isaiah to help her. The teacher asks her what else she can do to find the correct information she needs to close her breach, and she decided to search for a broader topic: "mid-segments." She tries it in the conference and finds what she is looking for:

> **Teacher**: So, what is the strategy that you ended up using?
>
> **Student**: I rephrased it.
>
> **Teacher**: You looked for a broader topic. When you started narrow, you were caught in a trap.

Here, the student learns from the teacher that searching for answers to her own questions can be tricky. If you search for a keyword that is too narrow, it can lead you down a rabbit hole to more confusion, so searching for a broader topic might help. This is a typical pitfall when students begin to ask their own questions and search for answers on their own. But, before the end of the conference, the student has an epiphany: Learning how to learn independent of the teacher's direction isn't really that hard.

> **Student**: I will look in the trapezoid section and, in the future, change my topic and look for a broader rewording. So, this is what my conference was about?
>
> **Teacher**: It is nothing earth-shattering, but you started stuck, and you are now unstuck.

THE HOLE IN THE WALL: HOW CAN TEACHERS HELP STUDENTS LEAD?

Student freedom is a scary idea for both kids and teachers—unless it is all you have left to work with. This was the case in Naina's and Whitney's Algebra and Environmental Studies classes. Most of the students in these classes were overage and had failed these courses multiple times, which they needed to pass to graduate.

It would be imperative to the ethos of the whole school to undo this logjam of repeat seniors stuck in these classes so the rest of the students could see that learning and advancing can happen at Green. Everyone was at a loss as to what to do in these two classrooms.

Naina describes the crisis:

> In November, the principal came in. Once again, I couldn't even get through my mini-lesson with the kids. The kids were saying, "Nothing is going on, This is boring." They were interested in deflecting. They would just joke, joke, joke, and deflected and interrupted me constantly. The kids, of course, were unwilling to give me anything and essentially continued to be in charge of the situation by deflecting, joking, and opposing each other until the bell rang. I turned to the principal. Nobody knew what to do.

Nobody knew how to pivot these classrooms—but lessons learned from the "hole in the wall" experiment by Sugata Mitra helped solve the problem.

Mitra placed a computer with Internet access into the side of a wall in a remote village in India to see what would happen.[2] Children gathered around the computer, and over time, they taught each other how to use it. Students taught themselves how to use Google and Google Translate and, eventually, taught each other English. Mitra calls this Minimally Invasive Education (MIE).

The principal suggested giving the students a real-world problem to solve. The idea was to create a pedagogy in which students self-organized and taught each other and solved a real-world problem—in this case, the problem of having to pass the New York State Regents Exam, which students needed to do to graduate. Teachers would enter the classroom, drop a bunch of old exams on the desks, and tell the students to Unison Read the Regents Exam, breach on the concepts they need to study, and solve their breaches together. The teachers would give them computers and laptops hooked up to Wi-Fi. And then, the students were left to it for three weeks.

Naina prepared the launch of this project. Naina wrote a list of the negative leaders in the class and paired each negative leader with a positive leader (some kids who were simply less negative than others were designated as positive leaders). Naina entered the classroom and called the pairs to another classroom so that she could work with them on setting up their teams.

With all teams chosen, she got a piece of paper and, while drawing, said, "Now, you will take out a sheet of paper and draw a matrix with a longer-left column filled with rows titled 'gist.'"

Naina explains what happened next:

Naina: Everyone got a copy of a Regents. We watched the students read a Regents question in Unison. The matrix came in.

Principal: The students breached, and their gist was something about osmosis [see figure 6.1].

N: It was about the fact that a membrane is semipermeable. It was a diffusion question.

N: They were debating about what the gist was, what they should be able to study from that question. I remember the kids mocking the process because they were not able to figure it out. But what they were talking about was content. They were discussing the concepts of diffusion, saying things like, "I think it has to do with a cell or a cell membrane." The kids rolled their eyes at us and got so mad: "See, we still don't know."

1 The cell represented below produces oxygen.

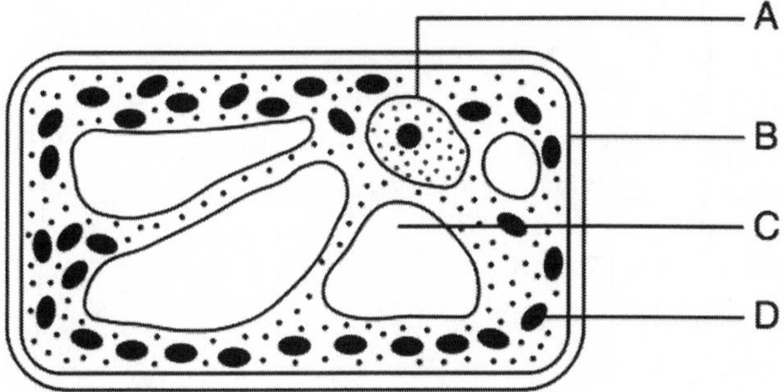

Which structure allows the passage of this oxygen to the environment?

(1) *A* (3) *C*
(2) *B* (4) *D*

Figure 6.1.

Principal: I was like, "No, keep at it, this is great, you are grappling with the content!"

N: They didn't see that because they just wanted someone to tell them the answer.

"The hole in the wall" experiment, called Responsibility Teams at Green, includes more adult scaffolding than the principal had originally envisioned and more than what Mitra had experimented with. Nonetheless, it shows the power of teachers giving total control to the students. When the students were given a problem to solve, as well as the proper resources and student-led protocols for learning, the kids in Naina's class got to work almost immediately.

It sounds like a soft landing for this story, but it was a huge transition from what was happening before. The students embraced the challenge and took responsibility for their own learning. They acted intentionally. Most of those students went on to pass their Regents exams that year and graduated. The school implemented these Responsibility Teams in every classroom the following year.

Passing state exams with a high score is an equity issue, especially in a state like New York, where students must pass the high school state exams in core subjects to graduate and get into many state colleges. Taking and passing this behemoth of a state test, with a high score in every subject, needs to be the expectation for each and every student, regardless of what reading level students come into high school with. Students who don't know the material in the disciplines—and, more crucially, can't read the test—won't pass the state exams and graduate from high school.

The Responsibility Team protocol gives students agency over the information within the constraints of a learning institution. Ultimately, in the case of courses that culminate in a standardized test, the Responsibility Team protocol is about teaching learners to identify what they need to know in order to be successful.

The bureaucratically driven (as opposed to teacher and/or student) classrooms in US high schools, which culminate in a statewide standardized exam against which both students and teachers are evaluated, do not allow teachers or students the time or the space in a school program that is needed to become critically conscious learners. Therefore, there is a great need for classes devoted solely to critically conscious learning, in order for students to receive a balanced education.

ENGENDERING A CRITICAL CONSCIOUSNESS IN WRITING AND READING CORE CLASSES

Teacher and philosopher Paulo Freire writes the following in his book *Pedagogy of the Oppressed*:

> There is no such thing as a neutral educational process. Education either functions as an instrument that is used to facilitate the integration of the younger generation into the logic of the present system and bring about conformity to it, or it becomes "the practice of freedom," the means by which men and women deal critically and creatively with reality and discover how to participate in the transformation of their world.[3]

Writing is a social action. The written word lives on after death, starts revolutions, ends wars, heals broken hearts, saves lives, and gives voice to the oppressed. The written word has the potential to create global change.

For the most part, writing is not taught as a social or cooperative action. Writing is normally treated as dead. Writing *happened*. The student takes notes, writes essays, and uses writing to demonstrate learning. The "audience" is almost always the teacher.

For the writer to be able to write with intention and develop a voice, the topic *and* genre must both be within the writer's control. Genres serve the writer's (or speaker's) intention. For a writer to achieve his or her intention, a writer must be able to make maximal use of a genre and its features, or even create a new genre, if needed.

In the Writing Share classrooms, students display their drafted ideas on paper in a genre of their own choosing, receive feedback, and then revise their piece.[4] The Writing Share neatly encompasses all of the Five Principles of Freedom and supports student autonomy and voice in their purest and most concrete expression. Every student takes writing as a core class every year at Green, where they write three times a week for a total of 210 minutes.

During writing time, students can write on topics and in genres of their own choosing. To help students to develop their own critical consciousness and form their own unique identity through writing, students also take a core reading class all four years, during which students are exposed to and choose to read a multitude of genres. In reading classes, students learn how to interpret a wide variety of different topics and genre features.

At the end of each writing period, all the students gather around the document camera for the Writing Share. A "Share Calendar" ensures all students have an opportunity to share once a month. The class provides the author with valuable feedback. In the Writing Shares, the author hears whether or not their draft is achieving its intended meaning.

The daily procedure is the same for each Writing Share. The writer walks up to the front of the classroom and places the writing draft on the document camera, positioning it so everyone can read it. Once the writer gets everyone's attention, she begins by telling the audience about her writing piece, making sure to specify its purpose and audience, and requests general responsive or specific feedback.

The writer reads the piece out loud. The audience reads along critically. At the end of the reading, the writer will ask: "Do you have any comments, questions, or suggestions?" The writer seeks to learn the answer to the question, "Am I achieving what I am meaning to say in this piece?"

The audience gives the writer feedback on how the written piece might be better understood or received by the readers. At the end, the writer says, "Thanks for listening," and the audience replies, "Thank you for sharing," and everyone claps. Learner intentions and the audience's interpretations drive the share and determine the teaching points. The teacher's role is to facilitate the "actor/interpreter"[5] cycle and help students learn how to give and seek quality feedback.

The theory of intentionality and the importance of critical reading both help explain why the Writing Share is so powerful. When a person acts intentionally by writing or speaking, it sets into motion this actor/interpreter cycle of communication:

- "Intentionality is one face of a two-part complementary process. The other face is interpretation. In the construction of every intentional act or utterance, *cultural patterns of interpretation* that will be necessary for communication are also engaged. Every speaker is also at times a listener. Although intentionality is expressed for others, it is also personal. One of the two basic constituents of intentionality is a psychological mode that packages personal meaning for public consumption. The interpretive exercise is a challenge, requiring one to understand the inner life of another from public expression."[6]
- In a sense reading requires every reader to become an actor; the reader has to "interpret" the lines he or she reads just as an actor has to "interpret" the lines for an audience, by uttering the lines with the correct expression.[7]
- When people achieve critical reading, they develop a "new conscience of what a text *could have meant* or *could mean* to a putative reader" because before this stage, "readers frequently fail to consider how texts could be understood or misunderstood by readers other than themselves."[8]

Over time, students learn how to critically read texts and judge whether or not they think the author used the genre features in a way that best served the authorial intention. Students "play" with genre features and authorial intentions in reading; this helps students be more playful with their interpretations of their own and each other's writing.

The following examples of Writing Shares demonstrate how much critical reading and reflection takes place in reading and writing classes at Green. As students take an active part in the actor/interpreter dynamic implicit in the Writing Share format, students develop more critical consciousness. In almost every Share, the writer learns something unexpected from the audience, usually relating to how their writing piece did not achieve exactly the reaction they intended.

Deon (name changed) is a black male student. He wrote his piece in part as a response to Amy Tan's short narrative piece "Fish Cheeks" and a class discussion around lived experiences and telling about them in written word. The teachers took the time to delve into how the character, an Asian woman, experiences a sense of shame in her culture brought on by the dominant culture of America (white Christians) and how the inner conflict is developed through the author's craft choices.

At the end of the discussion, the two teachers, Jeanne Zonneveld and Tim Bredl, asked who could relate to the feeling brought on by this story, and everyone raised their hands. When the teachers asked if anyone would be interested in playing with this idea or genre, a few students (Deon being one of them) raised their hands and started composing drafts.

Here is an early draft of what he composed, where he played with genre and started changing it into a poem (see figure 6.2):

Here is how Deon set up his audience for the Writing Share:

> **Deon's Purpose:** To let people know how I feel about black male teens and how they're being treated by everyone—to say we're all human, we're all the same.

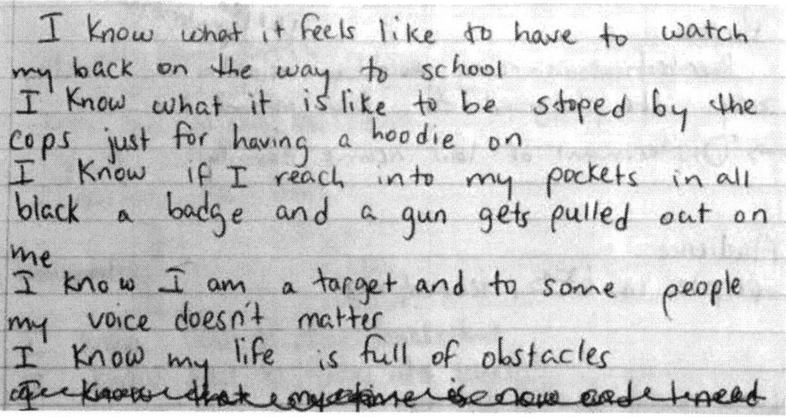

I know what it feels like to have to watch
my back on the way to school
I know what it is like to be stoped by the
cops just for having a hoodie on
I know if I reach into my pockets in all
black a badge and a gun gets pulled out on
me
I know I am a target and to some people
my voice doesn't matter
I know my life is full of obstacles
[illegible]

Figure 6.2.

Audience: Black male teens

Audience Reaction Desired: To feel aware and feel good about being black

Genre: Poem

Feedback: I want perspectives on different people's experiences.

After the writer read his poem to the audience, the audience responded. In a familiar twist that often occurs in the Writing Shares, Deon's audience, who were all students of color, didn't necessarily respond to his writing the way he had intended. They weren't sure his writing fit the norms of the genre, interrogated his assumption, and weren't convinced that Deon achieved his intention for the piece.

Mata: I feel like this isn't a spoken-word poem.

Deon: Why not?

M: The way you're reading it and the way you look.

Kyla: It's not formatted like a poem.

M: I know it doesn't have to rhyme, but there's nothing that really . . . I don't know.

Gabriela: What type of feedback do you want?

D: How do I adjust it?

Britney: I think you might want to do more research on this, because how can you be sure that every black male feels like this?

G: I really like the part where you say you feel like a target.

Crystal: I think you should ask people, older people, to see if they've been through or witnessed being stopped because of their color.

Tim: Tagging onto that, talk to who you know, and young black women, for different perspectives.

Eden: I think you should talk to the ones who are insecure about being black, who deny who they are.

D: I want to relate to them.

M: To say that black people are targeted.

K: Do you know what your overall theme is?

M: I can help you.

C: When you read this, I felt borderline being informed how teenagers feel being on the streets. If that's your purpose.

To help Deon solidify his purpose and intention for writing the piece, students suggested Deon interview older black people, women, people who have been stopped because of their color, and even those who are insecure about being black and deny who they are. They asked him to interview people to find out more about the different perspectives and biases implicit in his topic before revising the piece.

Students were quick to report where they thought the writing piece was insufficient (e.g., not fitting the genre form), confusing (what is the intention?) or unconvincing (how do you know all black males feel this way?). This reflexive response allows students to engage in a deep conversation around the issues they care about. As is the case in so many Writing Shares, the audience's responsive feedback forces the writer, Deon, to heighten his own critical awareness of the issues so that he is able to get the response he is looking for to his written words.

This next Writing Share is connected to three readings from Jeanne Zonneveld's Reading class:

1. A personal essay/list by Roxane Gay, entitled "How to be Friends with Another Woman"[9] from her book *Bad Feminist*. The class dug into what she was conveying about ideas perpetuated about women and her reason for writing this piece.
2. The teacher, Jeanne, also wrote and shared in response to this about a car crash she had gotten into, and how her father's offhand comment in response was, "This is why women shouldn't drive," and how it had really demoralized her.
3. A student, Asha (name changed), was also reading *Simon vs. the Homo Sapiens Agenda*, which is about a boy who is gay and blackmailed by a friend who finds out and is threatening to out him. The main character struggles with his identity as a gay male who presents or acts as a heterosexual male until he is outed and comes to terms with who he is.

All three of these readings resonated with Asha, which influences her writing. She sets the audience up for the Writing Share by preparing the audience to think about her intention for the piece and seeking feedback on whether or not she achieved her intention.

> **Purpose:** To show that people can be treated differently because of gender.
> **Genre:** Opinion (need help)
> **Audience:** Ladies and parents
> **Audience Reaction Desired:** Agreement

Asha: What can I add?

E: I feel you should relate it to yourself.

M: I feel like what E said, but I also disagree. They don't like when their kids have sex early, but are you talking about age?

E: Gender.

A: Yeah, gender.

M: Even in movies, it comes across that way, that Dad is proud when his son has sex.

C: I'm not persuaded that much, because you should go more in-depth about different cultures and different families. My family is like that. I would have been beaten up. It depends on your family.

K: The culture.

Teacher: I would look for something to add to the writing. You write, "Dad is going to be overprotective." Maybe use words like "controlling" and "uncomfortable." Other adjectives to describe dads.

K: I don't think it's only dads that are overprotective.

Teacher: What action do you want your audience to take after agreeing with you?

A: I guess maybe help see what parents are doing wrong and change the way they parent.

Teacher: Then look into research about sexual education from homes: How does that impact teen pregnancy, STDs, etc.? That would make me more open-minded.

K: If you're looking for a mentor text, I wrote about persuading teens not to have sex, but you can use it.

C: What's your perspective?

E: I would also say boundaries. It doesn't matter. So, talk about boundaries.

A: That's it?

M: Parents make it seem that sex is a bad thing, and this is why they don't educate their kids and then they end up pregnant.

E: I agree with M and disagree.

D: You should get different people's perspectives, like M's feelings, or other kids' feelings on it.

K: Talk about how people with overprotective parents who are strict; if their parents are too strict, it might cause kids to rebel. Research that.

Teacher: Maybe focus on the country—the US is not the same as other countries with sex ed.

In most Writing Shares, the author experiences an unexpected twist like this in how the audience responds to their drafted piece that can be attributed to the "cultural patterns of interpretation" that come into play when sharing writing in front of a live audience. The audiences' reflective responses to Asha's and Deon's pieces, and their suggestions, are similar: Get different people's perspectives on the subject, research and go into more depth about cultural differences and families, and consider the desired audience response.

The Writing Share is about more than developing a critical consciousness and understanding cultural patterns of interpretation of meaning; it is also something close to a daily form of therapy, where students listen to one another, give feedback, and, thus, develop empathy.

Students expand their "in groups" by learning about each other in these Writing Shares. Students write about their siblings, death, sickness, love, hate, suicide, politics, murder, abuse, abandonment, adventure—any topic they want. As students express their innermost feelings and thoughts to their audience of peers, and become open to critical feedback, they become better writers, develop their sense of selfhood, and discover a safe place to connect with others in the school community.

It is necessary to emphasize that the Writing Share would never have succeeded at Green if students weren't actively encouraged to work from a place of freedom, responsibility, and autonomy. The school could have purchased scripted curriculums that divide up writing content into genre units to study, or bought a step-by-step learning sequence, which asks the students to answer the curriculum developer's end-of-unit questions. The school could have purchased leveled reading units to study. The school could have asked the curriculum leads to write essential questions for each unit and do the backward planning for the class.

Educators must be careful that their own actions do not get it the way of students acting intentionally. Anything the teacher directs, creates, or disseminates can serve to silence the student's actions, voice, and mind. The Learning Conferences, Responsibility Teams, and Writing Shares and reading classes liberated students to act autonomously and with responsibility.

NOTES

1. David R. Olson, *Psychological Theory and Educational Reform: How School Remakes Mind and Society* (Cambridge, UK: Cambridge University Press, 2003), 145.
2. Sugata Mitra is a professor of Educational Technology at the School of Education, Communication and Language Sciences at Newcastle University. He is best known for his "hole in the wall" experiment, and he is widely cited in works on literacy and education.
3. Paulo Freire, *Pedagogy of the Oppressed* (New York: Herder and Herder, 1972).
4. Cynthia McCallister, "'The Author's Chair' Revisited," *Curriculum Inquiry* 38, no. 4 (September 2008): 455–71.
5. Feldman, 1999, 319; Janet W. Astington, David R. Olson, and Philip David Zelazo, *Developing Theories of Intention: Social Understanding and Self-Control* (New York: Psychology Press, 1999).
6. Feldman, 1999, 317; Janet W. Astington, David R. Olson, and Philip David Zelazo, *Developing Theories of Intention: Social Understanding and Self-Control* (New York: Psychology Press, 1999).
7. Olson, *The World of Paper*, 108–9.
8. Ibid., 135.
9. Roxane Gay, "How to Be Friends With Another Woman," August 1, 2012, https://www.google.com/amp/s/roxanegay.tumblr.com/post/28510427080/how-to-be-friends-with-another-woman/amp.

Chapter Seven

Fight

It was necessary at Green to overcome both teachers' and students' tendencies to prefer the educational status quo, which generally prioritizes student compliance and undervalues student autonomy and responsibility for one's own learning. Principals and administrators can best offset this tendency by displaying the Principles of Freedom in action, in the classroom, through the deployment of the innovative practices and approaches discussed in this chapter: Rule #23, Keepers of the Culture® (KOC or Keepers), Promise Cards, and KOC class.

Rule #23 is: "Provide leadership to encourage fellow students to follow established school policies and practices." This rule works because students respond better to a peer asking them to do something than to a directive from a teacher. In verbalizing their own needs and supporting those of others, students help create a "we-ness"[1] *identity in their classes and become the primary agents of change in the classroom.*

The Keepers of the Culture®[2] *is a group of students, elected by their peers, who provide leadership and support to students with multiple principal referrals. In addition to modeling appropriate behavior in the classroom, Keepers also attended the principal's behavior intervention meetings, as student allies.*

Gradually, these intervention meetings began to be called Promise Card meetings, because during the meeting, with the support of the principal and the Keepers, the disruptive student fills out a Promise Card, which acts as a record of the student's commitment to change.

The Keepers concept was next expanded into a civics course, called "the KOC class." The KOC class took over the Promise Card meetings from the principal. KOC Promise Card meetings helped build empathy and prosocial behaviors across the school as students helped, shared with, and informed each other in these meetings. Moreover, students who changed as a result of the help they received in KOC returned to help others and became loyal members of KOC themselves.

The Promise Card and KOC meetings highlight student intention and the act of handing control over to the student to develop his own change narrative. Students become very motivated when they see how their goals become their strengths and feel good when they change their behaviors and become part of a healthy group dynamic. There are no bad kids, just behaviors that get in the way of learning and cooperating—and behaviors can be changed.

It became very clear very quickly that students and teachers would need tons of support to embrace a pedagogy of freedom, all the time, every day. Traditional schooling practices tolerate low expectations for students and prioritize students' compliance over their autonomy of mind and voice. Living the Principles of Freedom would require everyone to fight against these traditional habits and processes that keep people conforming to this status quo, and, ultimately, keep students' minds oppressed. Everyone would need to learn how their own habits and processes (and coping mechanisms) were largely shaped by years of being part of an oppressive schooling system.

To change, all of the systems in the school needed to be re-envisioned in a way that would work against adults' and students' tendency to conform to the status quo. Students and teachers would need to be able to first identify, and then confront, their own impulses to fall back on doing what is familiar and "safe." Every student would need to change old beliefs and habits of mind in order to embrace the Principles of Freedom.

Convincing both groups of kids and teachers that the students already have the ability to develop the skills to be critically literate and take responsibility for their own learning would be the hardest part of this overhaul to carry out. As part of this pursuit, the students would need to help build up one another's confidence and leadership skills.

It can be a lonely fight for any school leader who wants to implement a pedagogy of freedom. The school principal is the gatekeeper in every school, and therefore, they have to be aware of, and prepared to engage with, opposing voices. Any change in staff and student beliefs and behaviors will happen if the school principal can defend the practices with theory and demonstrate them in practice.

As described in-depth in chapter 3, within the first two weeks of school, the principal, together with the students, established the Classroom Responsibility Ladder. This gave students six supported chances to adjudicate on their actions in the moment, inside of the classroom. On-call teachers entered classrooms at a moment's notice to cover for the classroom teachers to ensure that the learning formats continued despite disruptive behaviors, protecting everyone's right to an education. With the On-Call teachers taking over the learning formats, the classroom teachers could conduct side-by-side classroom behavior conferences with students.

Teachers averaged two or three of these conferences per day—and this is a conservative estimate. The principal conducted behavior and academic interventions with students and families on a daily basis. These were positive shifts in the right direction, but it was not nearly enough. Students were still doing things that got them suspended. Even with two deans, two assistant principals, and the principal actively working on behavior, it still wasn't enough manpower to keep up with the number of referrals, and the number of suspensions was high.

But—the high suspension rate was actually a good sign. It meant that teachers were addressing disruptive behaviors. It also suggested that more support was needed to help create a loving, supportive, and rigorous classroom environment that would create a sense of belonging and keep students engaged inside the classrooms and out of the hallways. To that end, several more innovations were put into practice that placed *the students* in charge of their destiny.

RULE #23

Teachers posted a big poster with Rule #23 on it at the front of every classroom: "Provide leadership to encourage fellow students to follow established school policies and practices." All of the student responsibilities are important, but Rule #23 goes directly to the heart of the idea of students being the primary agents of change in a school.[3]

The rule works because students respond better to a peer asking, "Can you speak in a quieter voice please?" or "Can you all come to my share now?" or "Carlos, you aren't listening to me when I talk. Can you stop talking and tell me what you think?" as opposed to a directive from a teacher. Rule #23 illustrates Michael Tomasello's theory that children want to enforce community or social norms because those standards help them create their group's "we-ness" identity (which will be discussed more in this chapter).

Rule #23 helped Sira become a leader, as illustrated in the following exchange.

Principal: What did you think of Rule #23 when you first came to Green?

Sira: I did not like it. I felt like I did not come into this school to help other people but just myself. So, it was really hard. I would give reminders after reminders, but I still had so many peers around me that wouldn't listen or participate. Now, I think I am good at bringing people into the group and helping them because I am a leader.

Principal: What do you mean when you say, "I am a leader"?

S: I have leadership qualities. I can tell someone, "This is wrong when you do this." Like, "Do this instead." I can help others out.

Principal: Were you always like that? From the beginning, when you got to the school? What changed you?

S: I started to focus more on what others wanted. I have grown as a person. I can tell people I am a leader because I have that quality.

Principal: What is the quality?

S: Leadership.

Principal: Which is what?

S: For me, it is telling them when they are wrong and when they are right and also lifting people up.

Principal: I remember you being upset about Rule #23 because you didn't think it was your job to help others. What other people did was not your business. You didn't want to snitch on other people. Like, you said, "I work by myself." So, how did you change? You don't talk like that anymore. What happened? How did you overcome that, Sira? You said, "I am a leader." I love that.

S: I feel like, over the years, I saw myself getting involved in things I did not want to be involved in. That's the way I felt. I needed to step back and think about what I wanted to be as a person. I had teachers and peers tell me, "You've grown as a person. You are not like how you used to be in ninth or tenth grade." And also, I was coming from middle school, and I was trying to figure things out with the way we do things at Green and the Ladder. It was mad confusing. I felt like, over the years, I started to understand and realize what was right. That's how I feel like I became a student, realizing what is right and what is wrong. I can help people out.

What Sira did not articulate, however, was that backing each other up was hard to do. Everyone needed to make sacrifices, and to be courageous and persistent, so as to give their peers the time they needed to adapt to such massive change. For more intensive student-student support, the Keepers of the Culture®[4] was created.

THE KEEPERS OF THE CULTURE®

The Keepers of the Culture®[5] (hereafter "Keepers") would be an elected group of students who would provide leadership and support to kids with multiple principal referrals. Here is how the Keepers started:

- The principal sent out a student survey that asked, "Name four students in your grade, group, or class who you believe will defend the culture of the school and the students' rights to learn."
- The principal met with those students and confirmed their commitment to a leadership role.

The initial idea behind Keepers was for these students to provide leadership inside the classrooms. Within a few weeks, the principal decided to also invite the Keepers to her office to attend her principal behavior intervention meetings.

PROMISE CARDS

During the principal behavior intervention meetings, the student creates a Promise Card. The Promise Card records and makes public the student's commitment to change. If the goal of the Keepers is to help fellow students to show leadership and follow the school's norms and practices in the classrooms, then it seemed a logical next step to have Keepers be student allies at the principal's intervention table. When the student allies joined the principal's behavior intervention meetings, these meetings started to be called Promise Card meetings.

THE KOC CLASS

At the end of the year, even with the added support of the Keepers in the classrooms and the Promise Card meetings with the principal, the suspension rate continued to rise. To address this, in the principal's second year, the Keepers concept was turned into an official civics course, titled, "the KOC class." The KOC class took over the Promise Card meetings from the principal. The KOC classes conducted, on average, up to nine Promise Card meetings a week—or about one thousand KOC Promise Card meetings every year, a tenfold increase over the previous year.

KOC Promise Card meetings helped build empathy and prosocial behaviors across the school as students helped, shared with, and informed each other in these meetings. Students who participated in these meetings expanded their friendship groups, and teachers observed many students abandoning their old friends for new, more supportive friends whom they met in KOC.

Many students attended over twenty KOC Promise Card meetings over the course of their high-school careers. Students who changed as a result of the help they received from other students in KOC returned to help others and became loyal members of KOC themselves. The next sections show how and why Keepers, or KOC Promise Card meetings, worked.

ERIC AND THE KEEPERS

When Eric arrived at Green, he found himself in some serious trouble. He started a fight that resulted in the police coming to Green. There were several injuries and major suspensions as a result of this altercation. When he returned from his own long suspension, the principal sent Eric to develop a Promise Card with the newly formed KOC class.

After many meetings, Eric became a member of KOC to help others benefit from the same help he had received. Eric was a senior when he was interviewed for this book, and he admits that, even as a senior who was about to graduate, he still asked for KOC meetings because he had more behaviors he wanted to change before he graduated. The principal started out by asking Eric if he thought KOC had helped the school transform:

> **Principal:** What is your perspective on KOC? What would you want to tell people about it? How did it help you? Do you think it helped?
>
> **Eric:** Yeah, it did. When I first joined KOC, I felt like KOC was a group of students who had good behavior, attendance, and stuff, but I had to realize that KOC wasn't about good attendance and good behavior because all the people I had KOC with were a group of people who did not have good attendance or good behavior. KOC was a group that took on the responsibility to hold people accountable for their actions.
>
> When we brought students in the classroom to talk about their absences or behavior or stuff like that, it was more like, "I do the same things that you do, so how can we make it better?" or "Let's work out somethings that can help you get to school on time," "Why don't you talk to your teachers so you can discuss why you are failing this class," or "Why don't we set up a time where we can all come together to talk about why your acting this way"?
>
> **Principal:** Why do you think it worked?

E: I feel like it was beneficial just because it was peer-to-peer. It wasn't like, just, coming from the teacher. You know how they have a position that is superior to ours in a way. It was like they were just talking, and like "Oh, you should do this" or "Maybe your teacher is mad because. . . ." Everyone just felt really comfortable speaking, and it was beneficial. It all depends on the kids, however; if they wanted to take it seriously or not.

Principal: What happened if they didn't take it seriously?

E: They would have to keep coming back, and then they would change it.

Principal: I think you would go out and get the kids too, so they felt a sense of belonging at some point. I remember kids hanging outside the KOC waiting around for you.

E: I did that, like, twice myself—I asked for KOC.

Principal: Even while you were on KOC.

E: I do it now!

Principal: You do it now?

E: Yeah, after I got suspended, and it was the first Promise Card I had to do. I felt good because there were no teachers around, and it was, like, "Alright, you don't have to tell them." It was, like, people helping me, like, "Hey, I do this, so why you don't try it?" Like, if teachers try to tell me something, I am going to get mad, like, "Why you telling me? You not my mom." But with KOC, students will talk to you about how to avoid getting in trouble. After awhile, you keep getting meetings, and you start to notice the change—you don't really notice it's happening; it's not like big, but when you go to your next meeting, they'd be, like, "Do you do this?" and you would be, like, "No, I stopped doing this," and so they cross it out, and then you would have less write-ups, and your grades start getting better, and you have good attendance. It just, like, helps you change.

Principal: Why do you keep asking for it now, Eric? What are the reasons?

E: Sometimes, in KOC now, I will ask for it if we don't have any kids. I will be, like, "Yo, when was the last checkup I had?" I am trying to get all my behaviors off by the end of this year. I got two behaviors left; that's talking and walking around. I don't think that last one is going to change, but I'll try (see figure 7.2).

Principal: The multiple iterations are what is important—you see yourself improving, and that you have been working on it.

If you peel back the layers of KOC protocol, you can see how the KOC group process ultimately depends on students *sharing* stories with each other, *informing* each other of the norms, holding kids accountable to their promises to change, and *helping* by offering up strategies to change.

These acts of altruism each day in the KOC classes led to the creation of a cooperative and loving culture at Green. What Eric describes here is how many students felt about KOC: Essentially, it is a form of therapy. The fact that a student can talk about her problematic behaviors with a group of supportive peers in a confidential setting is extremely beneficial. Eric is an advocate for KOC because the change narrative process helped him change for the better. Eric's story is also a reminder about one of the forgotten purposes of schooling: to prepare children to be functional adults.

DANTE AND THE KEEPERS OF THE CULTURE®[6]: CREATING WE-NESS[7]

No one, including Dante, thought Dante would graduate. Dante is an example of how students decided to give back and help others change. Here, Dante helps a younger freshman student, Michael, revise his Promise Card (see figure 7.1). Michael got into trouble almost every day for play fighting. When Michael became agitated during the meeting, it was Dante who opened Michael up by sharing his own story arc for Michael to use for guidance.

Here is a transcript of a KOC meeting with Jacquil (eleventh grade), Anna (tenth grade), Steven (tenth grade), Michael (ninth grade), and Dante (twelfth grade).

Michael: I was just playing around.

Jacquil: It didn't look like you were just playing around.

Teacher: [*to Michael and the Keepers who witnessed the incident outside at lunch*] From your perspective, did it look like they were playing, or was it a serious altercation?

J: It didn't look serious. It was play fighting. [*Turns to Michael, who has his old Promise Card in front of him and is looking down at it.*] What do you consider it? Because you were laughing.

M: I don't know, because I was just walking, and I got hit with a belt.

Anna: You were having fun.

J: You were laughing.

Steven: This is why we don't let people play fight, because people will take it seriously.

Dante: I don't know how you play with a belt and have fun at the same time.

A: The fact is that you were having fun. You were laughing. If it was serious, you would not have been laughing.

J: And then a belt?

A: Don't act like it's his fault because it is both of your faults.

M: Alright, alright, can you stop attacking me now? [*Biting his fingernails*]

Group: We are not attacking you. We were there, and we want you to think about and admit what really happened. You are not in trouble. We want to help you.

D: [*Pointing his pen down at Michael's Promise Card, figure 7.1.*] What do you think you can fix about this? I used to do the same exact thing. I used to ask for a bathroom pass, bust open the gym door, and play ball for the rest of the period and come back to class drenched in sweat. We didn't have KOC when I did this, so they just sat us all in a big meeting and said, "You all gotta get your stuff together." But now, what I feel is that you are a freshman. You are fourteen years old. I understand why you doing all this. But, when you see that you got a lot of things to lose, you won't be able to do none of this. Like when you in my position, like right now, I am about to graduate in two months. I'm, like, in heaven right now. Right? Like, I did all my stuff. I got all my shit together. And now, I don't have to worry about none of that. That behavior is going to cause you stress bro [*points to the behaviors part of the Promise Card*], and if you fail ninth grade, you might not graduate. What can you do to fix this?

M: [*Now with the pen in his hand.*] I think my main behavior is retaliation, I'm not gonna lie.

Promise Card

Name: Mike Evans
KOC Dates: October 14, 2014, January 21, 2015 w/ Mom and Mrs. Decker

Behavior that gets in the way of learning and getting along with others:
Talking in class about other stuff/basketball
Eating and drinking in class
Side Conversations
Walking around
Interrupt the teacher for a worksheet, a pen, to use the computer
Argue when someone says something to me that I don't like
Play fighting or retaliation
Argue when on the ladder

Social Contract violated: #1, 5, 10, 11, 12

Promise: I promise to change my behaviors.

Things I can do to change: I will talk about basketball outside of school at Town House after school program. When a teacher tells me to do something, I am going to do it right away. I promise I will not be off-task and disrupt other students when walking around the classroom. I am going ask another student a question instead of the teacher in a kind way.

Conditions If Promises Are Broken: I will accept the ladder, I will go to detention, **KOC Meeting**

Figure 7.1. Promise Card

> **D:** Like with the belt thing. I understand that. I would have gotten mad too. If someone "belts" into you like that, all you gotta do is walk away from them and be like, "Yo, I am not in the mood for this." You wanna be like, "Don't even hit me," but don't do it, don't even approach them with none of that.

Dante sympathized and empathized with Michael by sharing his own experiences. What is so powerful about this scene with Dante and Michael, and so many others like it, is that these KOC meetings allow this "he is me" feeling to develop.[8] This "he is me" attitude of identification with Dante allowed Michael to relax and learn that he wasn't alone. From this point on, he was able to name his primary disruptive behavior that gets in his way: "Retaliation."

The group would then continue to help Michael revise his transformational narrative and make a promise to change. It was this example that made the principal decide the students should completely take over the principal interventions. The kids were simply better at it.

At first, many educators cringe when they see how uncomfortable students are when they are asked to list out and identify all of their maladaptive

Promise Card

Name: Eric Ramirez
Date of KOC:10/7/15, 10/28/15, 11/10, 1/14/2016, 3/14/16, 7/25/16, 10/24/16, 11/21/16, 6/7/17

Behaviors that get in the way of my learning and getting along with others:

- ~~Playing around #5~~
- Late after lunch sometimes #1
- ~~Gets hit with pens and complains (talking off task throwing) # 5~~
- ~~Yelling at people in front of him because he feels like he has no respect #5~~
- ~~Name calling "Pimple face" to Maria One time~~
- Sucks teeth when aggravated #10
- ~~Complimenting people "Yo Randy you're so sexy" #5 - Says he doesn't do it anymore~~
- ~~Cursing "They're making this bullshit up" "What the fuck" "That's bullshit" #5~~
- ~~Throwing things at others #5~~
- Misuse of technology - With phone
- ~~Walking out of class (sometimes)~~
- ~~Flaming back~~
- Takes time to go to class
- Talking back to Tyler

Social Contract violated: 1, 3, 4, 5, 6, 7, 9,10, 22, 23

Promise: "I promise to change these behaviors"

Things I can do to Keep my promise:

- Go straight to class before lunch
- When I get hit with something I will talk to the teacher after class

Conditions If Promises Are Broken:

- Call home
- KOC
- No gym during lunch

- Electronic Signature: ERIC RAMIREZ

Figure 7.2. The Urban Assembly School for Green Careers

behaviors that get their way of getting along with others and being successful in school. Often educators (not the parents—parents love this process) who watch this process reactively assume that providing the opportunity for students to think about their own actions and how their behaviors can be helping or hindering their ability to get along with others is somehow pathologizing or hurtful to the student.

All kids want to belong, but they behave disruptively or uncooperatively, which leads the group to push them out. Listing the behaviors first and comparing them to students' responsibilities makes the rules of belonging explicit and gives the kids an opportunity to help each other adhere to those rules. Thus, listing and identifying behaviors is empowering, not pathologizing. Listing the maladaptive behaviors helps students become more prosocial by allowing them to develop their skills to be mindful of their actions in the moment, in order to be in control of their own actions in the moment.

The Promise Card and KOC meetings also highlight student intention and the act of handing control over to the student to develop his own change narrative. Students become very motivated when they see how their goals become their strengths and feel good when they change their behaviors and become part of a healthy group dynamic. There are no bad kids, just behaviors that get in the way of learning and cooperating, and behaviors can be changed.

Without a doubt, students at Green needed the thousands of therapeutic behavior-support opportunities put into place so they could learn how to be part of a healthy group dynamic. With that said, it was interesting to observe how and when students hit their stride. Dante and Eric hit their turning points in KOC. Sira needed classroom Rule #23 to take on a leadership role. Naya needed the Classroom Responsibility Ladder. Others needed a behavior conference once a month. Having a number of innovative techniques available helps students find the right approach that works best for them.

PRINCIPAL RESIDENCIES: FIGHTING TYRANNY AT THE TABLE

At Green, the urgent need for change meant that there would need to be time set aside to discuss theory at length with teachers. The principal decided that the professional development would need to focus on the students. Adult learning was going to have to happen in the classroom, alongside the students. To begin changing the failing school, it was important for the principal to immediately get into classrooms and spend time training the students and the teachers in the theory and the practice in what are called "principal residencies." The principal would say to the teachers, "Just watch me, watch the kids with me, take tons of notes, evaluate me against the rubrics, and let's talk about it and plan the next steps."

The professional development lead and the principal met once a week to plan the weekly principal residencies. The school hired two substitute teachers to be available on learning lab[9] days so that teachers could easily leave to attend a learning lab or residency. Every week, teachers took responsibility and figured out what learning lab, residency, or lead teacher classroom they would immerse themselves in.

MaryAnne (name changed) and Eli describe how embedded principal residencies flip the script on traditional adult learning practices in schools by helping teachers notice the intricate interactions between students and teachers that can keep students' voices oppressed.

> **MaryAnne**: Your principal lab sites and residencies where you modeled for us and allowed us to know what to look for in student/teacher interactions, which then allowed the wrangling to focus on deeper ideas grounded in pedagogy epistemology, rather than just tweaking maneuvers in a narrow way, which some coaching can feel like. It removes a lot of "stuff" that can come with teaching and makes way for more authentic discussions of theory and practice, which I believe helps teachers internalize the kinds of thought processes they would benefit from while making decisions in the classroom, as opposed to just "do this, not this." Teaching is inherently social, and you are constantly working within layers of social dynamics, yet we don't really train teachers how to do that and be reflective in the moment of teaching.

> **Eli**: It was the distributive leadership you did, and actually getting into the classroom and showing what you expect from your teachers and seeing the difficulties in the classroom with our kids and being able to work with that.

The principal benefits from the different perspective provided by going into the classroom and feeling the responsibility of the teacher in the classroom, rather than merely observing and telling teachers what to do. The principal residencies are about taking over the responsibility for change in the classroom and trying to figure out how to make the needed changes with the teacher, in the moment-by-moment dynamics of the classroom experience.

ELOISE: OVERCOMING THE TYRANNY OF SILENCE

Often the biggest threat to freedom of voice is the people in the room who try to silence it. This is why the principal would conduct lab sites and residencies in classrooms: She wanted to teach students (and staff) how to fight tyranny at their tables.

In some cases, the students who silence others at the table are obvious. This kind of person is usually the first to talk and the first to answer questions—someone who will dominate the entire conversation, interrupt others, and even call people names.

Then, there are others who are quiet and know how to navigate the social waters a little differently. In a classroom, it's important to look for the "silent silencer," because this kind can be more dangerous to freedom than the noisy ones. In addition to spoken and written language, nonverbal language cues communicate intention. If educators neglect to coach into and respond to the nonverbal social actions, it can do serious damage to a student group.

On one occasion, the principal walked into a reading classroom and noticed a group of students sitting together, poised to read—but rather than beginning to read together, everyone sat silently. The principal looked closely at the nonverbal silencers and immediately took over the group to coach the teachers about how to fight tyranny at the table.

"Hi guys. How's it going? I am going to just take over this group for now, and the teachers are going to watch me and take notes. So, where were you?" The group members showed absolutely no emotion, and two students shifted in their seats a bit. Something was up in this group dynamic. Turns out, they could decode words well. When they read in sync, it was so fast that the principal lost track of the meaning:

"Wait, breach! You read 'demolished,' and no one breached. Do you know what demolished means?"

One student looked at the principal, then looked down, and over to a student named Eloise, who said, "Yeah, we know what 'demolished' means. Let's keep reading."

"Wait. Eloise, are you sure everyone in your group knows what it means?" said the principal.

Annoyed, she replied, "Yes. We know already. Let's read!"

"Wait. What? How do you know, Eloise, that your group knows what the word means?"

"Because they didn't breach on it! Yo, this is mad stupid and slow, can we just continue to read now?" She looked at her group, the girls looked at her, and they all began to read.

"Whoa! Wait. No. We still have this breach to resolve."

Eloise looked at the principal and said, "What breach? We didn't have a breach, *you* did. We told you we know the word, and it's time to move on."

"I am a part of this group, and I am not ready to move on. This breach is not resolved."

The principal looked at Francis, the girl who looked up at the principal when she breached, and asked, "Do you know what 'demolished' means?"

She nodded her head.

"What does it mean?"

Not a word came out of her mouth. She shook her head, admitting that she, in fact, did not know what it means.

The principal asked, "If you didn't know the word, then why didn't you breach the group, Francis?"

Eloise let out a big sigh and rolled her eyes again.

"Eloise," the principal continued, "you just let out a big sigh right at the moment that Francis was about to admit that she doesn't know what a word means. Do you know what that does to someone's confidence? If you did that to me when I breached, I would be so scared that I would never breach again! Can you imagine if you breached on a word and I was like, 'Oh, come on' and rolled my eyes and looked off to the side? How would you feel?"

"I wouldn't feel nothing."

"No one breached. This is a problem. Why aren't you breaching?"

Eloise and the girls didn't say anything. Eloise looked away to the side with an impatient look on her face.

"We can't let this go." The principal looked at Francis. "Why didn't you breach? Do you also know what the last two sentences said? Because you all read this so fast that I couldn't keep track of the meaning."

Francis didn't respond. The principal looked at another student, Aischa. Both shook their heads.

There were a few serious issues in this group dynamic. The group was breaking rule #2 and rule #3: "Breach and talk about it, and be promotive to the group." Eloise's behavior at the table was causing the girls' voices to be silenced, and no one felt comfortable breaching. When a group process brings up many issues like this, it is hard to decide which one to tackle first. The principal's first go-to action in a moment like this is to prop up the people who are the victims of the silencer at the table, to teach them how to resist being silenced.

"Francis and Aischa. Neither of you knew the word 'demolished,' nor did you keep track of meaning, and not one of you breached. When I asked you why not, you two didn't even use your voices to speak to me, you shrugged and shook your head 'no.' When I breached the group, Eloise didn't like it and tried to move on without me. Now, if I weren't the principal of the school, I would be totally intimidated by Eloise's behavior because it would make me feel stupid and feel like what I think and have to say doesn't matter. So, I wouldn't speak either! I go super silent when I feel like people at the table don't care what I am thinking, or don't care about what I have to say at the table."

After a pause, she asked, "So, what are you two going to do now?" But the students remained silent.

The principal tried again: "Let's start by breaching. And if Eloise makes you feel bad about it, call her out and tell her she is breaking rule #3. Don't let her stop you from getting smarter."

The principal looked at Eloise and asked, "What are you doing to do to make sure the other people at the table feel safe around you?"

"They feel safe. They are my friends." "They are not going to tell you that they don't feel safe because rolling your eyes and sucking your teeth is not open and kind behavior, and so they are going to work on being able to stand up to you when you do things like this that break rule #3. But, right now, I am going to tell you that you need to be more promotive and make sure they feel safe to breach and talk in this group."

They start to read again and skip over "demolish" again.

"Wait!" interjected the principal, and then Francis said, "Breach!" The group stopped reading and looked at her.

The principal said, "That was great! Francis said 'breach' in a really strong and confident voice. Then you all looked at her. Now, do you know what you can say to help her out? Say, 'What's your breach?'" No one said anything, so the principal tried again: "Go ahead and say it. 'What's your breach?'"

In unison, the students said, "What's your breach, Francis?"

Francis replied, "I don't know the word 'demolish.'"

A lot of this kind of intervention was needed to help the students learn how to breach with confidence and talk together to resolve the breach. Bullying behaviors at the table were the biggest obstacle, but once students learned how to uphold the norms, many felt safe to breach.

PROTECT STUDENTS FROM THE LESSON AND TEACHER CONTROL

The biggest problems teachers had with the mandate to empower students was keeping the lessons short and letting students choose their own texts. These two issues were difficult to overcome, but it was necessary to do so to protect students' freedom of mind in classrooms.

The newly revised lesson was supposed to be a ten-minute opportunity for the teacher to highlight a successful strategy used by a student, a grammar/syntax/content lesson, or a chance to help a student to analyze a mentor text. Many teachers at first refused to do these lessons, so the principal eliminated all didactic PowerPoint lessons. She told the teachers that all lessons needed to be centered on: (1) text-based student writing samples and mentor texts; (2) student lesson requests; or (3) content from YouTube, TED Talks, and the plethora of other educational websites that, for the most part, do a great job of delivering lessons to students.

Teachers resisted this mandate by locking up the laptops and only giving kids access to the textbooks in Unison Reading®.[10] Or even worse, they only gave students access to photocopied chapter pages for the kids to read. In response, teachers were told that students needed to learn how to choose their own texts based on their own breaches and needs. This was reinforced by the assistant principal, who set up a system whereby students could order books and texts directly from an online bookstore so they could read what they wanted and choose from a great variety of texts.

The use of mandates and the explicit banning of oppressive practices helped protect student agency, emboldened student responsibility, and maintained high expectations for student learning:

- When the Social Studies and Science teachers put pressure on the Writing teachers to teach the test essays in Writing, students were banned from writing content essays in Writing class.
- When the teachers began to give students graphic organizers, graphic organizers were banned from the classrooms.
- Whenever teachers lowered expectations for students and gave the student's worksheet packets, photocopied texts to read, or unearned high grades for writing that was well below level, another mandate was introduced to help students stay in control of their learning and to maintain high expectations.

The teachers who remained at Green trusted that students not only *could* learn, but *wanted* to learn, and that if they gave students sufficient opportunities to learn in high-impact learning formats, they would learn even more than the standards required because they would be learning subjects and concepts that they wanted to know about. As psychologist Edmund Gordon said on one of his visits to the school, "Students learn how to be knowledgeable at Green."

To conclude this chapter, let's read how Dan Grenell, a math teacher, conveys how he reconciled the need to teach content in teacher-directed lessons in a school that follows the Principles of Freedom.

> **Dan**: I am happy to let go of teacher-directed lessons, but there is still a part of me that asks, "How am I going to teach them content?" That will probably always be there unless I get some sort of lobotomy. For a long time, my lessons were "content-y." There are a lot of things wrong with that, and the first thing we know is that it doesn't work.
>
> **Principal**: Why doesn't it work, Dan?

Dan: Because you are talking to the middle of the class; like, literally four kids, maybe. The kids who have learned the thing you are talking about don't care; they want to talk about something else. And the kids that are not there in their learning progression don't want to hear what you are saying.

It is also about what we said earlier: Adolescents don't want to hear what an adult says. I have seen students in shares say things that I have said in mini-lessons with 100 percent engagement, and I was at 20 percent. It is just more interesting when students hear it from a student's mouth.

When I have had lesson requests, those are always high-engagement lessons. Even if they are content lessons. If you asked for it, and I am giving it to you, you want to hear it. But the other thing was that the problem with my content lessons is that I wasn't setting kids up for success at other times. Maybe I gave a few kids a certain nugget of information, but the next time they wanted to know that nugget, they had no tools to figure it out.

I think Whitney helped me do this when she had a regiment for lessons: One day a week, she did a content lesson, one day a grassroots lesson [a strategy culled from student Learning Conferences], and one day a resource lesson. Just having the structure there pushed me out of doing content. It's not that I didn't want to do these other lessons. It is just that when I didn't create a dedicated space for them; they weren't happening, so I started with that: content one day a week, resource/genre one a day week, and grassroots.

After doing that for a semester, it was obvious which lessons were meaningful and important and which ones were not. So, the semester after that, I did practically no content lessons. And tons of resources and grassroots.

The pendulum swung a little bit back the other way toward content because I was getting more requests, and there was more coming out of my conferences, and we talk about them as three separate lesson types, but there is a certain amount of interdependency between them. I would never do a resource/genre lesson where I am just like, "Here is a book and check it out and identify text features." When I do a resource lesson, it is through the content.

And often, I do all three at once. I had a conference with a student, and the student had this question and found this website that no one has ever seen before, and they found it useful. "Here is the content on it; what can we extract from this information?" They are not three separate categories.

There are times when one is more dominant than the other, but many times, I find all three types of lessons are happening in the same lesson.

That was a couple of pivots: their lesson times, or the dedicated space for each one. The other thing is there are not a lot of people actually looking over our shoulders. We have a lot of leeway to figure things out and to do this without Big Brother or some, like, oppressive administrator looking over our shoulders the whole time. We are very much a teacher community learning together, talking about the theory and trying to improve, because we want to improve the class. It's not because Maddie or Kerry is going to come in and observe.

Principal: I think people would argue with you on that point! Several people don't feel like they have leeway.

Dan: A lot of the figuring out was given over to us, which is empowering as a teacher. To be told, here is some theory, here is some stuff, but, like, you have a lot of control over it. The other thing is I think it has a lot to do with is what you believe in.

There is so much that changes within these formats. The conversations the kids have within these texts is not moored to anything. There is nothing restrictive about those conversations. I am not telling kids what to say. Maybe that is the issue because we are not restricting what the kids say or think. We are not telling kids what to say or think. It's unrestrictive from the student's side. Maybe from the teacher's side, it is a little more restrictive; this many minutes for this and for that.

NOTES

1. Michael Tomasello, *Why We Cooperate* (Boston: MIT Press, 2009) and Michael Tomasello, *Becoming Human: A Theory of Ontogeny* (Cambridge, MA and London, England: Harvard University Press, 2019).
2. Cynthia McCallister, 2018, https://cynthiamccallister.com/.
3. Rule #23 is on the student responsibilities page 18 in the New York City Department of Education's *Citywide Behavioral Expectations to Support Student Learning* book (see figure 2.3).
4. McCallister, 2018, https://cynthiamccallister.com/.
5. Ibid.
6. Ibid.
7. "Children do not only respect social norms, as is typically argued, due to the benefits of reciprocity and threat of punishment. Instead, they are sensitive from a young age to their own interdependence with others in collaborative activities—a kind of social rationality endemic to shared intentionality—and they value conformity to the group as a marker of group identity. These different forms of 'we-ness' are important sources of both their own respect for social norms and their enforcement of social norms on others." From Tomasello, *Why We Cooperate*, 45.

8. "From a young age, children also possess a kind of social rationality along the lines of what the philosopher Thomas Nagel proposes in *The Possibility of Altruism,* what we might call a 'he is me' attitude of identification with others and a conception of the self as one among many, leading to the impersonal view from nowhere." From Tomasello, *Why We Cooperate*, 56.

9. During a learning lab or lab site, a group of teachers get together in the classroom to learn from someone else. After each lab site, there is a scheduled time for teachers to debrief around the normative pedagogical standards outlined in the rubrics and talk about what they learned from the person who conducted the lab site.

10. Cynthia McCallister, *Unison Reading: Social Inclusive Group Instruction for Equity and Achievement* (New York: Corwin Press, 2011).

Chapter Eight

Pushback—and Growth

Administrators should not underestimate the power and influence of a deep-seated belief among teachers that some kids (most often, minority ones) simply cannot change or will not change, whether because of their socioeconomic status, unstable family structure, or disability. This assumption undercuts student growth because it posits students as either too victimized to be held to social norms, or too disruptive to respond to anything but strict teacher dominance.

The principal can effectively challenge this mindset by spending a lot of time in the classrooms, in "embedded principal residencies." As the example of the principal taking part in a Unison Reading group in this chapter shows, all students benefit from a challenging, yet supportive and inclusive, approach that respects their input and abilities.

A student-empowered, freedom-focused pedagogy requires teachers to give up most of their traditional notions of control. It takes time, support, and hard work for students to learn how to think and act for themselves—and it takes time, support, and hard work for teachers to learn how to implement a pedagogical approach that favors autonomy over control. Principals need to know how to create a vision and be able to show teachers and students how to achieve it, especially when implementing a counterintuitive pedagogy based on the Principles of Freedom.

"What should be contrasted with practice is not theory, which is inseparable from it, but the nonsense of imitative thinking. Since we can't link theory with verbalism, we can't link practice with activism. Verbalism lacks action; activism lacks critical reflection on action." —Paulo Freire, Pedagogy of Freedom

Despite the successful innovations and changes at Green, some teachers, coaches, and administrators simply refused to engage with these new, theory-based methods and continued to disagree with, and even flat-out ignore, them. They instead recommended practices from the old playbook, such as,

"Tell a student four positive things before addressing a negative behavior," and "A student should only focus on one behavior at a time." They continued to believe that "only the counselor can decide if a child can take one of their behaviors off of the Promise Card," and to ask, "How will a student know if their answers are right if a teacher doesn't tell them the right answer?"

Or, they will go so far as to label norms as white supremacist in nature and send the message, "black students shouldn't be expected to follow white supremacist norms." These reductionist, anti-intellectual, and reactionary statements perpetuate the belief that kids are not capable of acting intentionally and adhering to prosocial behavioral norms. These beliefs and attitudes only serve to keep standards low and maintain the socially oppressive hierarchy and pedagogy that led the school to fail in the first place.

"GROWTH MINDSET" STOPS AT "AT RISK"

There is this binary mindset among some in education, marked by a belief that kids either won't or can't change. Some people on staff at Green believed that kids could change, but they or their family members chose not to; or they believed that kids just could not change because of a disability or attribute (e.g., poverty, social status, trauma, etc.). Progressive ideas of "growth mindset" almost always stop at special education or in underperforming schools.

This fixed mindset that people place on "at risk" kids who misbehave or underperform academically interferes with student growth. Student development is undercut by either a sense of clinical exceptionalism (i.e., the students are seen as too victimized to be held to social norms), or of maximal control (i.e., the students are understood as too disruptive to respond to anything but unreflective adult dominance). People on staff often patronized kids because of their lack of resources and social status and did not expect children to perform or behave at the same high level as kids from more stable or wealthy families.

Why such low expectations for kids from low socioeconomic backgrounds (especially black and brown students)? Can't the children tell each other if they've changed? Who says that kids can't work on changing more than one behavior at a time, all of the time? Why can't students ask their own questions and choose their own texts? Why can't students be expected to use their cell phones appropriately, only for learning? Why can't they write on topics and in genres of their own choosing and give each other feedback for revision?

This struggle is partly due to the politics of recalcitrant school districts and the sociocultural beliefs that drive those systemic politics and, thus, affect student and teacher behaviors. Despite the disapproval and pushback from some camps, implementing a pedagogy based on theories undergirding the Principles of Freedom is not impossible in schools if the school personnel remain focused on the values of the Principles of Freedom.

The results of a coherent and consistent practice based on the Principles of Freedom will speak for itself. At Green, the suspension rate began to drop precipitously starting in the new principal's second year and continued to drop five years later. The graduation rate steadily improved from 39 percent in 2013 to 83 percent in 2017.

THEORY IN PRACTICE: MODELING FREEDOM FOR TEACHERS AND SUPPORT STAFF

School leaders can sit in their office analyzing spreadsheets and the daily attendance percentages every day. They can hire coaches to come in and teach teachers directly or purchase leveled-reading or scripted core-knowledge programs. But unlike those practices and programs, the Principles of Freedom are grounded in theories of mind that emphasize that individual learning is a social practice, as opposed to purely an individualized mental function. Since learning as a social practice runs counter to most pedagogical approaches, it was necessary for the principal to spend a lot of time in the classrooms, in what were called "embedded principal residencies."

DEVELOPING INTERSUBJECTIVITY IN AN EMBEDDED PRINCIPAL RESIDENCY

The principal sat at a Unison Reading table in a classroom with a large number of students who were learning English as a second language. The entire Social Studies department hovered around her, writing down everything she and the students said. The students breached on the word "canon," which was used in the text metaphorically to refer to an aspect of the Scientific Revolution.

The dictionary definition wasn't going to help the students. The students tried various strategies but were wrong each time. The principal let them struggle. To the right of her, one student turned to another student and started a conversation in Spanish. The principal breached the group and told the students that, by having a side conversation, they were not being promotive to the group.

Later, when the teachers and the principal debriefed on the lesson, the teachers asked her why she had reprimanded the kids for speaking Spanish. She didn't know what they were talking about. "What do you mean?" she asked. They referred to their transcripts and showed her what had happened. Her perspective of what had happened was completely different from the teacher's perspective. She thought the two students who started to speak in Spanish to each other were having a private side conversation about the word "canon," but the teachers saw the two students trying to use Spanish, their native language, to help them figure out the meaning of the word.

Either way, she told the teachers that the students broke Rule #1: stay in sync. If the two students were, in fact, using their native language, it was not inherently problematic, but regardless, they had to stay in sync with the rest of the group. They should have breached and said, "Wait a minute, do you need one of us to help you translate this into Spanish?" This is why it is important to create experiences that require teachers, students, and the principal to be intersubjective and work through the messy parts of learning how to be free: how to think, act, speak, and fight together.

Of course, principals do not need to wait until classes begin to model techniques for the teachers. While on-the-ground training is vital, it's wise to give teachers plenty of time and opportunities ahead of time to practice a freedom-based approach—and to model the approach yourself. For example, in her very first staff meeting with teachers, before school started in September, the principal asked the teachers to put her in some likely scenarios they would encounter in the classroom, so that she could model for them how she would handle it. The teachers had fun with this one and had plenty of likely scenarios for her.

Math teacher Whitney Fink decided to play a student named Selena (name changed), to see what the principal would do when she refused to come to her group's table for Unison Reading. Whitney learned something vital from watching the principal that first day together: The group must secure Selena's engagement as part of their group. This would be essential if the teachers were going to create a culture of freedom at Green.

The principal would not let Selena's group continue until the students themselves from Selena's group got Selena involved, even if it took all period, all week, or all month. This is how Whitney later described this moment:

> **Whitney**: I played Selena, and I was refusing to be part of the group. We were role-playing to show how this should all go. And [the principal] was just, like, "We do not learn in here until you are doing what you are supposed to be doing." She just would not let groups continue until they got the other kid involved. That was a hard but important moment for us because otherwise, I don't think we would have ever gotten all the kids at the table.
>
> **Principal**: What do you mean?

Whitney: So many of them were on the fringe. If we didn't force every student to take responsibility for all the ones on the outside, our best-case scenario was 50 percent would learn anything, because so many of them could choose to not be part of it.

TEACHER AUTONOMY AND PRINCIPAL MANDATES

Teacher resistance is a likely hurdle. If the principal makes an explicit expectation, teachers will challenge it. This is good. You cannot change if you do not feel challenged. Before this interaction, teachers all may have had different ways of dealing with a student refusing to join a group, but now they had a common understanding from which to act.

The word "mandate" is a controversial one. Teacher resistance to mandating the implementation of any format that takes away teacher control and gives students the agency and responsibility for learning is fierce. It became imperative to protect student's freedom of mind through mandating the pedagogy of freedom in a contract. The contract outlined the students' and teachers' responsibilities for every format during a school day. Teachers and students used these contracts as a rubric to evaluate themselves and one another for their adherence to their goals and aims.[1]

Along with the contracts, the principal mandated the classroom daily flow so that every student had, for example, the opportunity to spend twenty minutes a day in each class in Cooperative Unison Reading®,[2] share their writing twice a month in the Writing Share, spend one hour reading from their own texts, and one hour writing in topics and genres of their own choosing every day.

To offset teacher resistance to this mandating of protected space for students to practice freedom, the principal explained her approach to them: "I am not micromanaging your time. I am protecting the students' opportunities to learn how to learn independently. I am not micromanaging what you teach by giving you a scripted curriculum or a pacing calendar to follow and telling you to 'Be on unit nine by December.' I am giving you total autonomy of what to teach students by letting you decide what to do based upon your daily observations of students."

So then, why the controversy over mandates? The fact is, to be a student-empowered school, Green's teachers had to give up most of their traditional notions of control. Of course, this is not easy to do. It takes time, support, and hard work for students to learn how to think and act for themselves—and it takes time, support, and hard work for teachers to learn how to implement a pedagogical approach that favors autonomy over control.

THE EQUITY PIVOT: COUNTING THE AMOUNT AND THE QUALITY OF LEARNING MINUTES IN SCHOOLS

There is nothing more powerful in the fight for freedom than actually counting the opportunities students have to learn in the freedom-focused formats. But there are a hundred reasons that can eat up the learning minutes: the lesson goes over ten minutes; there's an assembly; a parent comes in to read to the class; student and teacher absences; school nurse and counselor visits; bathroom breaks; fire drills; early dismissals; snow day; holiday and birthday parties—and the list goes on.

Why count how the minutes are used in schools? What students do the most during the most minutes of the school day is what they will get really good at doing. If students spend most of their minutes engaged in interpretive discourse with others debating the meaning of a variety of texts, then they will grow skilled at thinking and using their voice and understanding other people's perspectives. If students spend most of their minutes sitting passively in a lesson, then kids get good at taking notes, memorizing, and learning what someone else thinks and doing what someone else dictates. If kids spend most of their school minutes doing worksheets, then they will be good at answering the teacher's questions.

If teachers start counting what actually happens minute-by-minute in school, it might become clear why students aren't doing well in school. Counting how the minutes are spent in schools and the number of opportunities students have to learn in high-impact learning formats is fundamental to providing a high-quality and equitable education.

Teachers and administrators reviewed the Unison Reading and Learning Conference records to count the number of opportunities each child had to learn each month in a high impact learning format. Getting these numbers back is the best kind of feedback. Often, teachers realize they haven't met with a student because this student skips class every time he is up for a Learning Conference or is somehow avoiding Unison Reading right before their eyes! What you find out by counting is that there are a hundred ways to hinder a student's opportunity to learn. Once teachers can see the problems that get in the way of a student's opportunity to learn, the teachers can work to solve the problems.

To create a clear vision, map out a clear plan, and be able to show students and teachers how to do it inside of the classrooms is vital to the success or failure of a school. The principal at Green had a reason for everything she did, and she wasn't afraid to talk about it or show what it should look like inside the classrooms. Principals need to know how to create a vision and be able to show teachers and students how to achieve it, especially when implementing a counterintuitive pedagogy based on the Principles of Freedom.

A LETTER TO FUTURE SCHOOL LEADERS WHO BELIEVE IN A PEDAGOGY OF FREEDOM

Dear School Leaders,

Be Clear and Explicit about Your Vision. Know the theory behind it, and the counter-theory, too. Distinguish the good theory from bad theory. Learn how to implement the theory in practice, and be able to model it, over and over again. Be able to talk about theory in front of teachers and in front of the district-level administrators. Be able to support every single action with theory. Know the practices that support a pedagogy of freedom—and know the practices that conflict with a pedagogy of freedom. It's your responsibility to America's children to be a scholarly pedagogue who is fluent in the theory and in the practice. Get yourself there. Settle for nothing less.

Create the Rules of the Game. A social contract is the school's normative beacon. When using a pedagogy of freedom, a social contract serves to protect students' freedom of voice and mind. Students and teachers use these social contracts as the embedded evaluation rubrics. Everyone uses the embedded rubrics to adjudicate their minute-by-minute actions in terms of the responsibilities outlined in them. Students, teachers, and administrators use these embedded evaluation rubrics to score each stakeholder's developing abilities and skills.

Lead the Change: Show, Don't Tell. Start with the person or people you are trying to empower: the students. Embed the professional development into the classroom practices. Beliefs and behaviors are hard to change, and talking about the theory with the teachers and the students in the actual action of the practice helps shift the culture of learning. Teachers may not be capable of understanding the concepts behind the principles of freedom and putting them into successful practice at first, so go right to the students. Students do understand the concepts behind a pedagogy of freedom. They may resist freedom at first, but students will embrace the principles of freedom more readily, and then will start to demand a freedom-based approach from their teachers.

Flip the Script: Shift the Power. Embed principals inside the classrooms. The principal's role is to show leadership where it counts, to teach the theory-to-practice relationship inside the classroom, where the action unfolds.

Hire Carefully: Fire Swiftly. Kids are vulnerable, and education has taken advantage of this in a way that has shut down their minds and voices. Move out teachers who oppress students' voices and minds and refuse to change. Many teachers come into teaching with a perhaps unconscious "savior" mindset, especially in schools with many "at risk" students. A pedagogy of freedom is about changing years of oppressive control-based practices in schools. If teachers are not prepared to confront their bias and identify and change their behaviors that oppress students' minds and voices, then they need to get out. Be prepared for teacher turnover, and consider it a good thing when these teachers leave. The reality is that there are many well-meaning teachers out there, many of whom will say they believe in a pedagogy of freedom but few of whom will ultimately act on such a belief. Sadly and surprisingly, students tend to be more flexible and open-minded than most twenty-five-year-old teachers (note to future self: hire former students to teach).

Students Are the Agents of Change in Schools. Students far outnumber the adults in the school. A principal will not be alone in the fight when the students are empowered to provide positive leadership and be the change. Students can rise to the challenge. They are the real change agents.

Don't Capitulate; Don't Cop Out. The American educational system at the national, state, and district levels still largely adheres to the same oppressive pedagogy and top-down management structures that make it difficult to implement a pedagogy of freedom. It's possible, but it requires a fight. A pedagogy of freedom threatens the oppressive power structure that employs many people. But all of the adults' actions in a school should be focused on preparing students to be critically literate and self-actualizing individuals. Be willing to lose your job over this; the kids deserve to learn how to be knowledgeable, self-directed, and free.

Sincerely,

A Principal of Freedom

NOTES

1. Rubric samples used at Green can be found at Cynthia McCallister, 2018, https://cynthiamccallister.com/.
2. Cynthia McCallister, *Unison Reading: Socially Inclusive Group Instruction for Equity and Achievement* (New York: Corwin Press, 2011).

Bibliography

Astington, Janet W., David R. Olson, and Philip David Zelazo. *Developing Theories of Intention: Social Understanding and Self-Control.* New York: Psychology Press, 1999.

Bruner, Jerome. *The Intentionality of Referring. Developing Theories of Intention: Social Understanding and Self-Control.* New York: Psychology Press, 1999.

Feldman, Carol Fleisher. *Intentionality and Interpretation. Developing Theories of Intention: Social Understanding and Self-Control.* New York: Psychology Press, 1999.

Freire, Paulo. *Pedagogy of Freedom: Ethics, Democracy, and Civic Courage.* Lanham, MD: Rowman & Littlefield Publishers, 1998.

————. *Pedagogy of the Oppressed.* New York: Herder and Herder, 1972.

McCallister, Cynthia. "'The Author's Chair' Revisited." *Curriculum Inquiry* 38, no. 4 (September 2008): 455–71.

————. *Unison Reading: Socially Inclusive Group Instruction for Equity and Achievement.* New York: Corwin Press, 2011.

New York City Department of Education. "Progress Report 2012–2013." https://data.cityofnewyork.us/Education/Schools-Progress-Report-2012-2013/cvh6-nmyi/data.

Mei, Lori, and Jennifer Bell-Ellwanger, Jennifer. *The Class of 2001 Final Longitudinal Report: A Three-Year Follow-up Study 2005 Report. New York City Department of Education Joel L. Klein, Chancellor. Division of Assessment and Accountability (February 2005).* http://www.nycenet.edu/daa or http://schools.nyc.gov/Accountability/Reports/Data/Graduation/Class_of_2001_Final_Longitudinal_Report.pdf.

Olson, David R. *The World on Paper. The Conceptual and Cognitive Implications of Writing and Reading*. Cambridge, UK: Cambridge University Press, 1996.

————. "Self-Ascription of Intention: Responsibility, Obligation and Self-C ontrol." *Synthese* 159 (2007): 297–314. DOI 10.1007/s11229-007-9209-2. Published Online: 10 August 2007. Springer Science-Business Media.

————. *Psychological Theory and Educational Reform: How School Remakes Mind and Society*. Cambridge, UK: Cambridge University Press, 2003.

————. *The Mind On Paper: Reading, Consciousness, and Rationality.* Cambridge, UK: Cambridge University Press, 2016.

————."A New Theory of Agency and Responsibility." Learning Cultures, 2014. https://www.youtube.com/watch?v=x5wwt7l8Lmc.

Steele, C. M., and J. Aronson. "Stereotype Threat and the Intellectual Test Performance of African Americans." *Journal of Personality and Social Psychology* 69, no. 5 (1995): 797–811. http://doi.org/10.1037/0022-3514.69.5.797.

Tomasello, Michael. *Becoming Human: A Theory of Ontogeny*. Cambridge, MA and London, England: Harvard University Press, 2019.

———. *Why We Cooperate.* Boston: MIT Press, 2009.

Vygotsky, L. S. *Mind and Society: The Development of Higher Psychological Processes The Development of Higher Psychological Processes.* Cambridge, MA: Harvard University Press, 1978.

———. *Thought and Language* (A. Kozulin, Ed.). Cambridge, MA: MIT Press, 1986.

World Economic Forum. "The Future of Jobs Report 2018." September 17, 2018. https://www.weforum.org/reports/the-future-of-jobs-report-2018 .

Index

About the Author

Kerry Decker Rutishauser has dedicated her entire professional life to eliminating oppressive schooling practices. Kerry completed her MEd in Educational Administration at Teachers College, Columbia University. For the past twenty-four years, Kerry has been a teacher, achievement coach, New York City school principal, and a writer. She has worked in PK–12 schools in Illinois, Kuwait, Wisconsin, and New York City and successfully turned around two struggling New York City public schools. Kerry continues to live and work in New York with her husband and four children.